Oxford Resources for the Caribbean

Primary Language Arts

CW01494411

Let's Leap!

Teacher's Guide

Imelda Vázquez Córdova

Editor: Anna Yeomans

OXFORD
UNIVERSITY PRESS

OXFORD
UNIVERSITY PRESS

Great Clarendon Street, Oxford, OX2 6DP, United Kingdom

Oxford University Press is a department of the University of Oxford. It furthers the University's objective of excellence in research, scholarship, and education by publishing worldwide. Oxford is a registered trade mark of Oxford University Press in the UK and in certain other countries.

© Oxford University Press 2025

The moral rights of the authors have been asserted

First published in 2025

All rights reserved. No part of this publication may be reproduced, stored in a retrieval system, transmitted, used for text and data mining, or used for training artificial intelligence, in any form or by any means, without the prior permission in writing of Oxford University Press, or as expressly permitted by law, by licence or under terms agreed with the appropriate reprographics rights organization. Enquiries concerning reproduction outside the scope of the above should be sent to the Rights Department, Oxford University Press, at the address above.

You must not circulate this work in any other form and you must impose this same condition on any acquirer

British Library Cataloguing in Publication Data
Data available

978-1-382-05215-3

978-1-382-05216-0 (print)

978-1-382-05217-7 (Kerboodle Book)

10 9 8 7 6 5 4 3 2 1

The manufacturing process conforms to the environmental regulations of the country of origin.

Printed in Great Britain by Ashford Colour Ltd

The manufacturer's authorised representative in the EU for product safety is Oxford University Press España S.A. of el Parque Empresarial San Fernando de Henares, Avenida de Castilla, 2 – 28830 Madrid (www.oup.es/en or product.safety@oup.com). OUP España S.A. also acts as importer into Spain of products made by the manufacturer.

Acknowledgements
The publisher and authors would like to thank the following for permissions to use copyright material:

Written by Imelda Vázquez Córdova and Anna Yeomans
Cover illustration: Kelly Caswell

Artwork by QBS Learning

Every effort has been made to contact copyright holders of material reproduced in this book. Any omissions will be rectified in subsequent printings if notice is given to the publisher.

The manufacturer's authorised representative in the EU for product safety is Oxford University Press España S.A. of El Parque Empresarial San Fernando de Henares, Avenida de Castilla, 2 – 28830 Madrid (www.oup.es/en or product.safety@oup.com). OUP España S.A. also acts as importer into Spain of products made by the manufacturer.

Contents

Introduction to *Let's Leap!*

Let's Leap! is designed to meet the requirements of all the Caribbean Primary Language Arts curricula from Year 1 to Year 7. It can be used with any Caribbean Language Arts curriculum and is suitable to use alongside any phonics system that you currently use.

Let's Leap! has been developed in order to help teachers engage students more in their learning, and to increase their success in meeting the learning objectives of their own Primary Language Arts curriculum. The course is based on three fundamental principles of learning:

1. We all retain information more effectively when it is linked to positive emotions, for example, interest, enjoyment, humour, empathy.
2. We all find information more interesting and engaging when it links to our own life experience and personal interests.
3. Everyone masters any skill most effectively by active learning. In the context of Primary Language Arts, this might entail reading, completing a task while listening, speaking in authentic speaking activities where there is a genuine exchange of information, and writing own ideas.

The course is divided into three sections:

1. The introductory years: Levels 1 and 2
   In these years, students are beginning to learn the skills needed for learning, and developing good learning habits. They will develop a love of learning and master the skills through materials that are fun, engaging, and accessible, to enable them to build the skills they will need throughout their education.
2. The development and consolidation years: Levels 3, 4 and 5
   During these years, students are developing all the skills they learned at Levels 1 and 2, and applying them in increasingly sophisticated ways to more and more complex materials. The focus is still on engaging and age-appropriate materials, so that students develop the skills to an increasingly higher level while enjoying the learning.
3. The expanding and test preparation years: Levels 6 and 7
   In these years, students are building on the earlier foundations, building confidence, expanding their skills to apply them at higher levels to an increasing range of more complex texts, and using more complex and wide-ranging language for an increasing range of purposes. This progression helps them to establish excellent foundations for the later stages of their education. They build their knowledge and understanding and gain practice in all the skills they need in order to succeed at tests and exams.
   In Level 7, a whole unit (Unit 9) is dedicated to provide advice and practice in the main question types students are likely to encounter in their exams. The wording of each question may not exactly match what they will see on their test paper, but the range of questions cover those found in the different PLA test papers. Answers to the test-style questions, and a writing assessment grid to mark writing tasks, can be found in this Teacher's Guide on page 55.

Active learning

Active learning puts the student at the heart of the learning, in contrast to a teacher-led approach, where the teacher leads from the front and imparts most of the information, while the students are mainly recipients.

In active learning, the teacher sets up an activity, ensures students have the language or other resources, and then monitors the activity while students participate in it. This provides ample and constant opportunity for formative assessment, as the teacher is free to observe and listen while moving around, monitoring the groups. The teacher checks understanding and prompts students to think or express themselves further by asking questions. The teacher thus has a good idea at all times of where each student is in their learning.

Key features of active learning:

- Strong focus on speaking and listening
- Pair and group work
- Maximum student-to-student talk
- Activities to encourage independent thinking
- Giving students ownership of their learning, for example by reflection and self- and peer-assessment
- Having all students involved all the time
- Motivational for students
- Easier for teachers than imparting information
- Integrated skills (all four skills, plus language, are included in every lesson)
- An active learning–formative assessment cycle, where you assess students continuously and unobtrusively as they learn. See more on formative assessment in the Assessment section on page viii.

Active learning activities include:

- Authentic speaking activities, where there is a genuine exchange of real information, such as students' own opinions, thoughts and experiences
- Project work
- Problem-solving activities
- Shared writing tasks
- Completing a task while listening
- Asking students to set the success criteria
- Encouraging students to reflect on their own learning: what they did well and how to improve.

Every page of the Student Book involves active learning activities. Activities are designed to be fun and engaging while being fully underpinned by academic rigour and current educational theory.

Every activity is linked to a specific learning objective, or to several learning objectives. These are shown in student-friendly language at the top of each page. New language is introduced in context as students encounter it in the reading texts, and they start to use it immediately in the activities. By participating in active learning, students gain confidence, which increases motivation. This positive cycle results in faster learning and higher attainment.

Classroom management

It is important to set up the classroom to encourage students to communicate with each other. You also need to be able to move around the classroom freely in order to carry out your monitoring and enabling role with all students. Moving around also means that you can encourage the students to engage with all activities. Here are some approaches to help you:

- If possible, arrange the seating so that students are facing each other, preferably in groups of three or four. The aim with active learning is to have more student-to-student talk than teacher-to-student talk. This is the approach used in the Student Book activities, and this seating arrangement facilitates genuine communication between students.
- Move around the classroom during activities. Try speaking from the back or the side of the classroom. This way, every student has you standing near them at some point, which increases focus and engagement. There should be no areas of the classroom where some students might feel less noticed.
- As you move around the classroom, listen to students, ask questions to check understanding and promote further thinking. See the Assessment section on page viii.
- Most activities should involve students working in pairs, groups or individually. They are interacting with each other, rather than directly with you, and your role is to monitor, observe and ask questions to promote further thinking. Try to avoid whole-class activities where you are asking questions to the whole class, and some students are putting up their hands to answer. With this approach, formative assessment is much more difficult, since you only establish whether the one student who answers has understood. If students are working together and you are monitoring, you can establish exactly who has achieved the learning objectives, and who may need extra support.
- Change the groups regularly.
- When grouping or pairing students, you may choose one of the following methods, or you may use all these methods at different times. They all have different advantages, with some disadvantages.
  - *Random groups,* for example when you number all the students and tell all the number ones to be in one group, and so on.

- ◇ Advantages: the groups will be mixed ability, so students can help and learn from each other; students may be outside their comfort zone, working with students they don't usually work with, so behaviour may be better.
- ◇ Disadvantages: some students may not work well together.
  - *Mixed-ability groups.*
- ◇ Advantages: similar to random groups, but you can group students who work well together. You can also split up any friendship pairings that may be distracting.
- ◇ Disadvantages: some higher-level students may become frustrated.
  - *Grouping according to level.*
- ◇ Advantages: students can work with others at the same level, so higher-level students are challenged, and those working at a lower level gain confidence as they work without the help of higher-level students; you can vary levels of challenge for different groups, for example, asking higher-level groups to produce longer writing or use more complex language, or supporting lower-level groups with vocabulary lists, writing frameworks or sentence starters.
- ◇ Disadvantages: some students may be demotivated being in a lower-level group.
  - *Friendship groups.*
- ◇ Advantages: these work well at the start of the year to put students at their ease; boost confidence and motivation.
- ◇ Disadvantages: students may be easily distracted; groups will work with the same dynamics as the friendships, with some students dominating, or some doing all the work, not participating, or trying to be funny.
- Encourage questions and predictions.
- Avoid error correction while students are speaking. Focus on the meaning of what they are saying and deal with errors in general class feedback.
- Allow students to use their home languages initially in speaking activities to build confidence. When they can speak freely and confidently, encourage them to speak in English. Encourage discussions about the similarities and differences between their home languages and English.
- Focused noise is good noise. If all students are engaged in a speaking and listening activity, group work or project work, there will be a healthy amount of classroom talking. You can hear what each student is saying by moving around the groups.
- If certain students show a lack of engagement, it is important to analyse the cause. You may be able to make the necessary changes to increase engagement. You could change the groupings or pairs, provide more support or challenge, ask questions to relate the topic to students' own experience, or adapt it to their interests.

About the course

The *Let's Leap!* programme of study

In order to develop the programme, all the Caribbean curricula were mapped, and a new set of learning objectives was developed to cover almost all the individual learning objectives in the individual Caribbean curricula.

The following table shows how the *Let's Leap!* resources correlate to your primary school structure, wherever you are across the Caribbean.

Let's Leap! level	Age group	Trinidad and Tobago	OECS	Barbados	Jamaica
1	4–5 years	Infant 1	Kindergarten	Reception	Kindergarten
2	5–6 years	Infant 2	Grade 1	Infant A	Grade 1
3	6–7 years	Std 1	Grade 2	Infant B	Grade 2
4	7–8 years	Std 2	Grade 3	Class 1	Grade 3
5	8–9 years	Std 3	Grade 4	Class 2	Grade 4
6	9–10 years	Std 4	Grade 5	Class 3	Grade 5
7	10–11 years	Std 5	Grade 6	Class 4	Grade 6

The wording of the individual learning objectives in the *Let's Leap!* programme of study (PoS) may not exactly match the wording of your individual curriculum, but the meaning of the words and the learning objective described will match the equivalent learning objective in your curriculum. You can find more detailed information on how the *Let's Leap!* PoS maps to your own curriculum from your local Oxford representative.

The *Let's Leap!* course covers the four skills of speaking and listening, reading and writing. The language skill is for use throughout the other skills. The language learning objectives are divided into vocabulary (everything to do with word formation (morphology), word classes, and vocabulary range) and language structure (grammar, syntax, how the words fit together into meaningful sentences in Standard English).

Learning objectives

As with your own curriculum, each skill is divided into a number of smaller, more specific individual skills known as learning objectives. The learning objectives show clear and consistent progression from one grade to the next. This ensures that there are no gaps in the learning. Progress in any individual learning objective is clearly measurable from year to year.

The learning objectives are written in full in the Teacher's Guides and are written in student-friendly language in the Student Books and Workbooks. This is so that both teachers and students can see how they are developing the skills through every activity.

Learning objective codes

The codes for the learning objectives work like this:

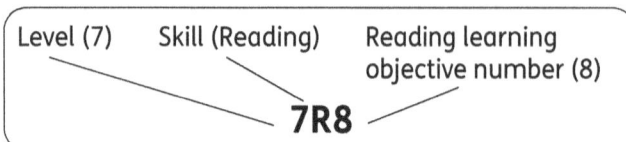

You'll find the full list of objectives for this level on page xviii.

Scope and sequence

In each Student Book you will find a scope and sequence chart (entitled 'Programme of study: Learning outcomes'). This shows how the learning objectives are spread across the nine units in each level. If students complete all nine units, they will have covered all the learning objectives in the curriculum.

Topics

Each unit focuses on a topic or theme. The topics are designed to be of interest to students in the Caribbean and to increase awareness of the wider world. When students study topics that are of interest to them, and of which they have some personal experience, they engage with the learning in a more meaningful way because they are able to bring their own ideas, opinions and experiences to the topics covered. When they are able to do this, they achieve the learning objectives more fully and they retain the learning more deeply because the new learning links to their own interests and experiences.

The texts and activities in each unit are all related to the topic, and the projects will synthesise the learning objectives in a group activity also based on what the students have learned. There is no requirement for students to learn topic information, instead the topics are the vehicles for developing the learning objectives in a meaningful and authentic context.

The topics are also designed to develop wellbeing and other valuable social and personal attributes important in Caribbean culture and in the modern world. Topics in the *Let's Leap!* resources also link to other curriculum areas, for example mathematics, science, music, geography, and personal and social care and wellbeing, so that you can integrate the Primary Language Arts learning with other curriculum areas.

Texts

The texts have been written specially for this series by Caribbean and non-Caribbean authors. They celebrate Caribbean themes and culture and are designed to be of interest especially to students in the Caribbean. Each unit has fiction, non-fiction or poetry which will engage students' interest in the theme, introduce new vocabulary and ideas, and provide a model or stimulus for students' own writing. The series includes texts in different Creoles and in English. The focus of the language and assessments is Standard English, but parity of respect is given to all local languages and the series acknowledges the wealth of Caribbean culture and literature available to students.

Reading

All texts are designed to develop the theme and exemplify the language points of the unit.

Reading at Levels 1 and 2

All the texts are intended to be read aloud by the teacher while students listen, look at the illustrations and begin to follow in their own books at Level 2. The content and interest level are appropriate for the age of students but they are not expected to read these texts independently. This is made clear in the Student Book and in the teaching notes for each unit.

As students work through Level 1, there are opportunities for them to apply their phonic knowledge to blend phonemes to read individual words or short sentences. This becomes more established throughout Level 2 where students are directed to read speech bubbles in fiction and some simple labels and captions in non-fiction texts. At each stage, the words they are reading are in line with the progression in their systematic phonics lessons. This means that they can apply their knowledge to decode words or they will have learned to recognise and read the high-frequency/tricky words.

To encourage students' independent reading, you could put together a selection of books on the unit theme and have these available in the classroom for students to browse and read by themselves or in pairs. Look for any texts that fit in with the theme from the graded reading books that students are using. Support students in finding texts that are at their own reading level so they can practise reading them independently.

Reading at Levels 3, 4 and 5

Texts can be read aloud by the teacher while students follow the words in their books. Students will move progressively towards independent reading by reading sentences, then sections or paragraphs aloud by themselves. Paired reading is encouraged, where students read in pairs, taking turns to read a sentence, verse or paragraph each. This enables peer feedback and builds confidence. You can move around the pairs monitoring all or most students' reading. This is much more effective than calling students up to take turns to read to you. It is not essential to hear every student read in every lesson, but aim to hear them all during a week. By the end of Level 5 it is expected that students can read texts independently. The complexity of the texts they can read independently may vary according to level or ability. The reading skills which students develop from Level 3 onwards include reading for explicit and implicit meaning, making inferences, predicting, analysing literary features, and making a personal response.

To encourage wider independent reading outside the classroom at Levels 4 and above, students will be taking home reading books or, if possible, accessing a library. You may like to have a 'Book club' session every week or fortnight, when students work in small groups and share what they are reading. They can talk about the book, give an informal spoken book review saying what it is about, what they liked about it, what they didn't like, and whether they would recommend it. This can develop into written book reviews at higher levels. Students can be encouraged to read whatever interests them, and to talk about it, including graphic novels or comics or magazines, to encourage reluctant readers.

Reading at Levels 6 and 7

It is expected that all students are reading independently at varying levels. Students can continue with the activities above to encourage their wider reading.

Speaking and listening

Since engaging students in speaking and listening is at the heart of active learning, speaking and listening are included in every lesson. Not only does this engage students and build confidence, but it enables you to know what they are thinking, and easily to assess their current level of understanding. Students who are reluctant writers can engage with concepts and achieve reading learning objectives through speaking, for example when responding to texts, or understanding literary features. For written tasks, by discussing answers to questions before sharing with the class, or discussing their ideas before writing a text, students gain confidence as they have the chance to try out different ideas with a partner and refine or develop their ideas.

Speaking and listening activities will result in more noise in the classroom, but you can ensure that this is engaged, focused noise, by moving around and monitoring the groups. This also enables you to teach students the important life skills of taking turns, listening to others and responding appropriately. The Student Books teach these aspects of speaking and listening explicitly too.

Creole and Standard English

The series includes texts in different Creoles and in English. The aim of the series is to acknowledge the important role that both Creoles and Standard English play in students' lives and in the life and culture of the Caribbean. At the same time, the series leads students towards the goal of succeeding in examinations conducted in Standard English. Effective communication skills have been shown to be a strong marker of future life success. By developing students' communication skills in this way, and exposing them to literature in both languages, the series prepares students to succeed wherever in the world life may take them, both at home in the Caribbean and in a wider global context.

For the language of instruction, you may wish to use either Creole or Standard English, depending on your students and your own context. The aim is to use whichever language of instruction will best help students to engage with the learning and master the learning objectives and they will do this best if they enjoy the lessons and feel that the learning is within their reach. As students progress, you will move more towards Standard English as the language of instruction, but at every stage of learning the parity of Creole is acknowledged. You may wish to explain certain language points or discuss certain topics in Creole, or encourage students to do so, if you feel this is more appropriate and if it enables them to express their ideas and opinions more effectively.

Assessment

Formative assessment

All the activities in the Student Books and Workbooks provide opportunities for formative assessment. Students can assess each other's work, which consolidates and increases their learning as they see what others have done. Every unit provides opportunity for self-assessment and reflection too, when students evaluate their own work and their own learning process. This enables them to take ownership of the learning as they decide themselves what they need to work on to improve.

When you are formatively assessing students during activities, good formative assessment questions you might ask include: *Can you say more? Can you give me an example? What exactly do you mean? How will you do/show/say that? How can you make that even better?*

Summative assessment

In each Student Book for Level 3 and above, there is a summative assessment every three units entitled 'Check your learning'. This covers the learning objectives of the previous three units. Instructions on how to use these assessments are provided. They can be used as classroom activities, or as more formal tests. It is recommended that a more informal, classroom approach is used in the earlier years, moving towards a more formal, test-like approach at higher levels to prepare students for formal summative assessments later on.

These assessments can also be used to adapt your plan for the next three units, to revisit any learning objectives that some students have not fully mastered.

Supporting students

If any students have not mastered a learning objective, or they need more support during activities, you can support them in a number of ways:

- Differentiation by task. This is where you give some students a simpler version of a task, for example, by asking them to write a few sentences about a topic, instead of a paragraph giving their opinion on the topic, or by identifying language features instead of using them.
- Differentiation by outcome. This is where students all complete the same activity, but you accept a lower level of outcome for some students, for example, they all write an opinion text, but some students write three points, while others write five and back up each opinion with an example or reason.
- Differentiation by support. You can provide vocabulary lists or sentence starters, or provide a writing frame where students fill in the gaps in a simple text. You can also provide support in mixed-level pairs or groupings, by encouraging higher-level students to support lower-level students through peer teaching. However, it is important not to over-use this approach, since it is important to keep higher-level students sufficiently challenged. You may also simply wish to revisit some activities in an earlier unit of the Student Books or Workbooks with some students to give them another opportunity to complete the activity and achieve the learning objective. You may need to provide some more examples of language points to help them to master the learning objective.

For students who exceed the learning objectives, or complete activities early, it is important to provide extension activities. The Student Books and Workbooks provide Stretch activities for this purpose. These can be completed individually, in pairs, or they can be used for all students as another classroom activity. Students for whom the work is too easy can be just as disruptive as those for whom the work is too hard, so it is essential to provide additional challenge for these students, using the three types of differentiation above. You can require more of them by making the tasks more challenging, the outcomes harder, or by providing less support and encouraging more independent learning, for example by asking for longer stories, more detailed text analysis, or independent research. Extension activities can be used as a reward, for example by having a box of interesting reading and writing extension activities in the classroom so that students can choose an activity if they finish classroom activities early.

How to use the Student Book

Each Student Book is made up of nine units. The course is designed to be covered over three school terms, with three units in each term. It is estimated that each unit, including the Workbook activities, will take approximately four weeks of teaching. If you complete the whole Student Book and Workbook, you will have covered all the learning objectives in the programme of study multiple times. Thus students will have had the best opportunity to achieve their learning goals for the year. You may find that your students work at a slightly different pace, but since all learning objectives are covered more than once, this will not affect their learning for the year.

Each unit is structured so that all lessons include elements of speaking and listening, reading and writing. Each skill leads into the next one and prepares students for the next task. Students engage with the topic by linking it to their own experience and sharing what they know and think. Texts for reading lead into further speaking and language work, which leads into writing. The projects bring the learning together in an integrated group activity where students practise all the skills they have learned in the unit.

Unit opener

This page orientates students towards the topic for the unit. The pictures provide a stimulus for discussion, and give students the opportunity to share their ideas, experiences and opinions. The Let's talk questions relating to the pictures give the teacher the opportunity to assess students' speaking skills and check prior knowledge of the topic.

Learning objectives

The learning objectives are written in student-friendly language on each page or spread in the Student Books. This is so that students can see what the aim of each activity is, and how it links to their progression in different skills. Students are more motivated when they can see the learning purpose behind any activity. All the student-friendly learning objectives for each activity in the Student Book link to the full learning objectives listed for each activity in the Teacher's Guide.

Glossary

Explains the meaning of new words as they occur in the text.

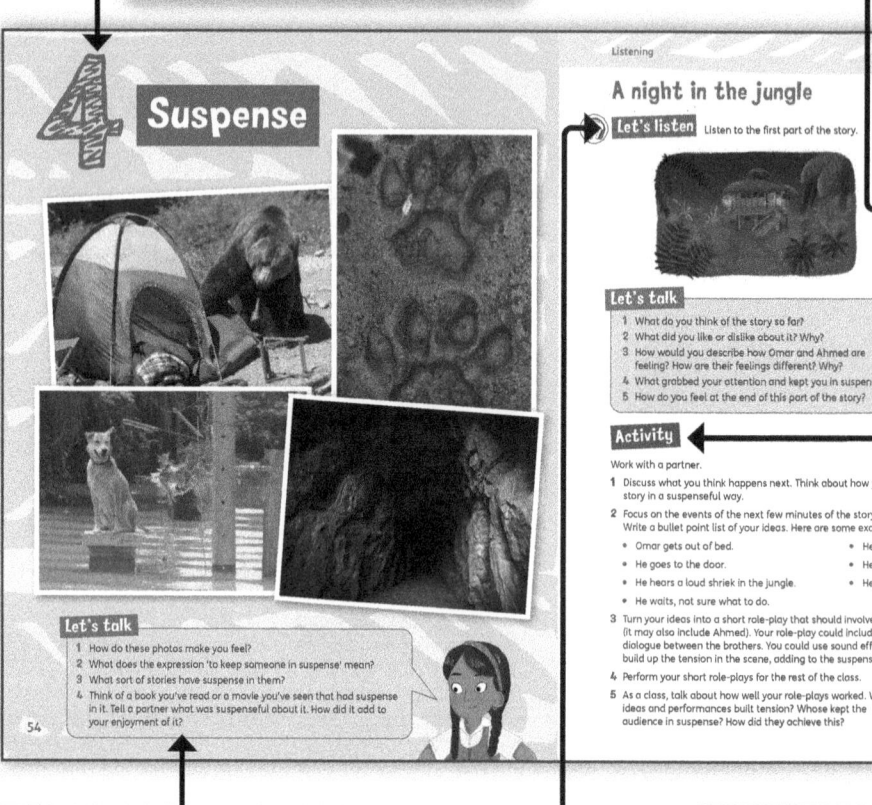

Let's talk

As discussed previously, speaking and listening are an integral part of every lesson. These features encourage all students to engage with the topic and the learning objectives at every level. Speaking activities are used for follow-up reading activities, and as preparation for writing activities.

Let's listen

Students develop their listening skills by completing tasks while listening to spoken texts. This enables the introduction of a wider variety of texts, for example, interviews, drama and discussions, among others.

Tip

Additional information or guidance specific to a skill, learning objective or language point.

Activity

Reading texts are followed by activities to develop different reading learning objectives. New language or literary features are followed by activities to develop understanding and usage of the form and function of the new language. Understanding and usage progresses from recognition, through controlled practice, to freer production.

Let's read

The Let's read sections introduce a range of different texts, with each unit focusing on fiction, non-fiction or poetry as its main text, but other texts in the unit may offer an example of a different text. Each text, while being engaging for students and focusing on the unit topic, also models the language covered in the Language sections. This is so that language forms or literary features are understood in a realistic and natural context.

Language

New language points are introduced, with examples. Further guidance is given in the Teacher's Guide on how to extend the language work to ensure that all students have understood, can recognise and use the new language. This new language includes literary features, or figurative language, for analysing and writing texts.

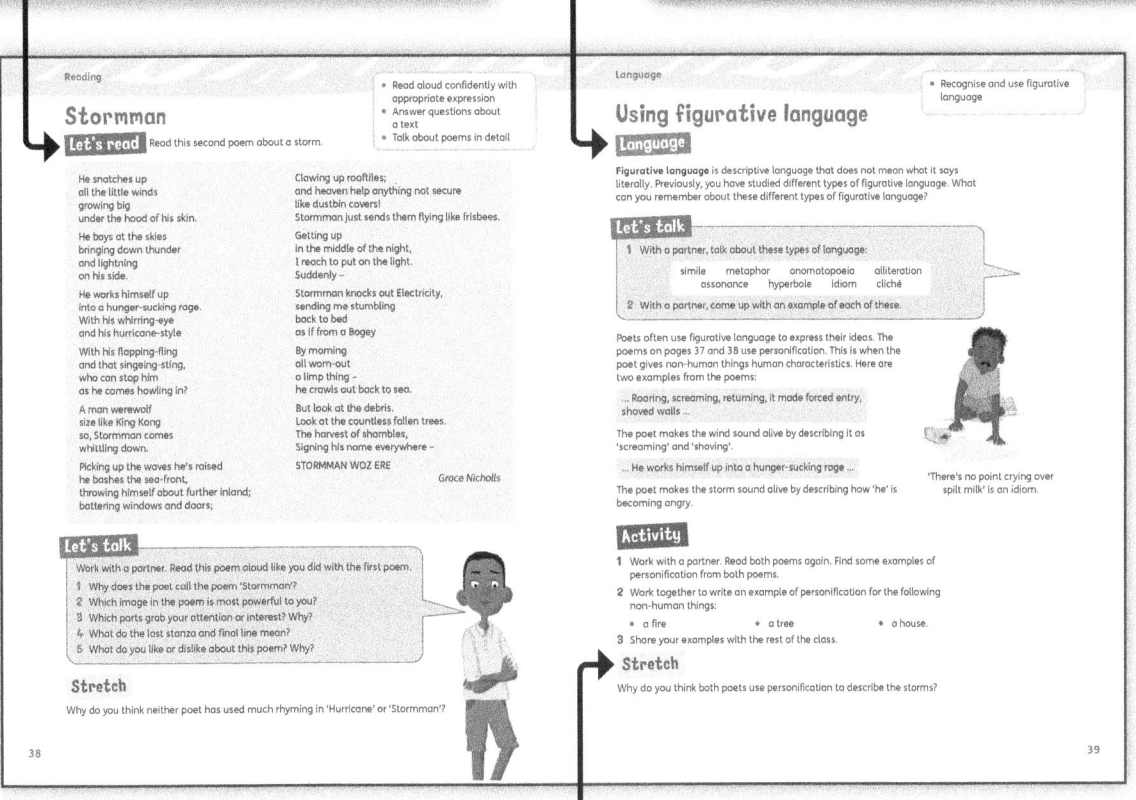

Reading

Stormman

Let's read Read this second poem about a storm.

* Read aloud confidently with appropriate expression
* Answer questions about a text
* Talk about poems in detail

He snatches up
all the little winds
growing big
under the hood of his skin.

He bays at the skies
bringing down thunder
and lightning
on his side.

He works himself up
into a hunger-sucking rage.
With his whirring-eye
and his hurricane-style

With his flapping-fling
and that singeing-sting,
who can stop him
as he comes howling in?

A man werewolf
size like King Kong
so, Stormman comes
whittling down.

Picking up the waves he's raised
he bashes the sea-front,
throwing himself about further inland;
battering windows and doors;

Clawing up rooftiles;
and heaven help anything not secure
like dustbin covers!
Stormman just sends them flying like frisbees.

Getting up
in the middle of the night,
I reach to put on the light.
Suddenly –

Stormman knocks out Electricity,
sending me stumbling
back to bed
as if from a Bogey

By morning
all worn-out
a limp thing –
he crawls out back to sea.

But look at the debris.
Look at the countless fallen trees.
The harvest of shambles,
Signing his name everywhere –

STORMMAN WOZ ERE

Grace Nicholls

Let's talk

Work with a partner. Read this poem aloud like you did with the first poem.

1 Why does the poet call the poem 'Stormman'?
2 Which image in the poem is most powerful to you?
3 Which parts grab your attention or interest? Why?
4 What do the last stanza and final line mean?
5 What do you like or dislike about this poem? Why?

Stretch

Why do you think neither poet has used much rhyming in 'Hurricane' or 'Stormman'?

38

Language

Using figurative language

Language

* Recognise and use figurative language

Figurative language is descriptive language that does not mean what it says literally. Previously, you have studied different types of figurative language. What can you remember about these different types of figurative language?

Let's talk

1 With a partner, talk about these types of language:

simile   metaphor   onomatopoeia   alliteration
assonance   hyperbole   idiom   cliché

2 With a partner, come up with an example of each of these.

Poets often use figurative language to express their ideas. The poems on pages 37 and 38 use personification. This is when the poet gives non-human things human characteristics. Here are two examples from the poems:

... Roaring, screaming, returning, it made forced entry, shoved walls ...

The poet makes the wind sound alive by describing it as 'screaming' and 'shoving'.

... He works himself up into a hunger-sucking rage ...

The poet makes the storm sound alive by describing how 'he' is becoming angry.

'There's no point crying over spilt milk' is an idiom.

Activity

1 Work with a partner. Read both poems again. Find some examples of personification from both poems.
2 Work together to write an example of personification for the following non-human things:
   * a fire
   * a tree
   * a house.
3 Share your examples with the rest of the class.

Stretch

Why do you think both poets use personification to describe the storms?

39

Stretch

These activities take students beyond the learning objective. They can be used with the whole class, or as an extension activity for those students who have already achieved the learning objectives, or finish the activities early. They can be done individually, in pairs or in small groups.

Projects

The projects bring the learning together in an integrated group activity where students practise all the skills they have learned in the unit. One project focuses mainly on reading and writing, and one on speaking and listening, with a particular emphasis on the performance speaking and listening learning objectives.

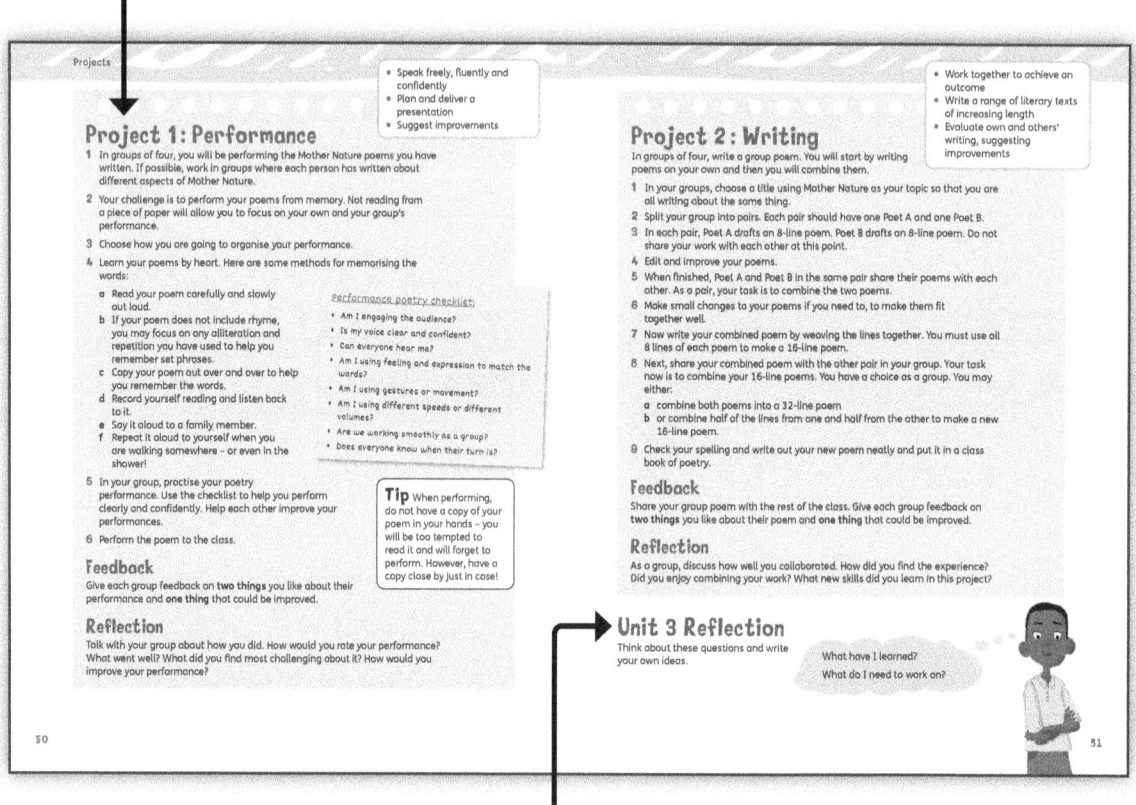

Unit reflection

Students reflect on their own learning at the end of every unit. This can increase their motivation as they think about what they enjoyed and did well, and you can gain valuable, at-a-glance information about their progress.

Check your learning

This covers the learning objectives of the previous three units. Instructions on how to use these assessments are provided. They can be used as classroom activities, or as more formal tests. It is recommended that a more informal, classroom approach is used in the earlier years, moving towards a more formal, test-like approach at higher levels to prepare students for formal summative assessments later on.

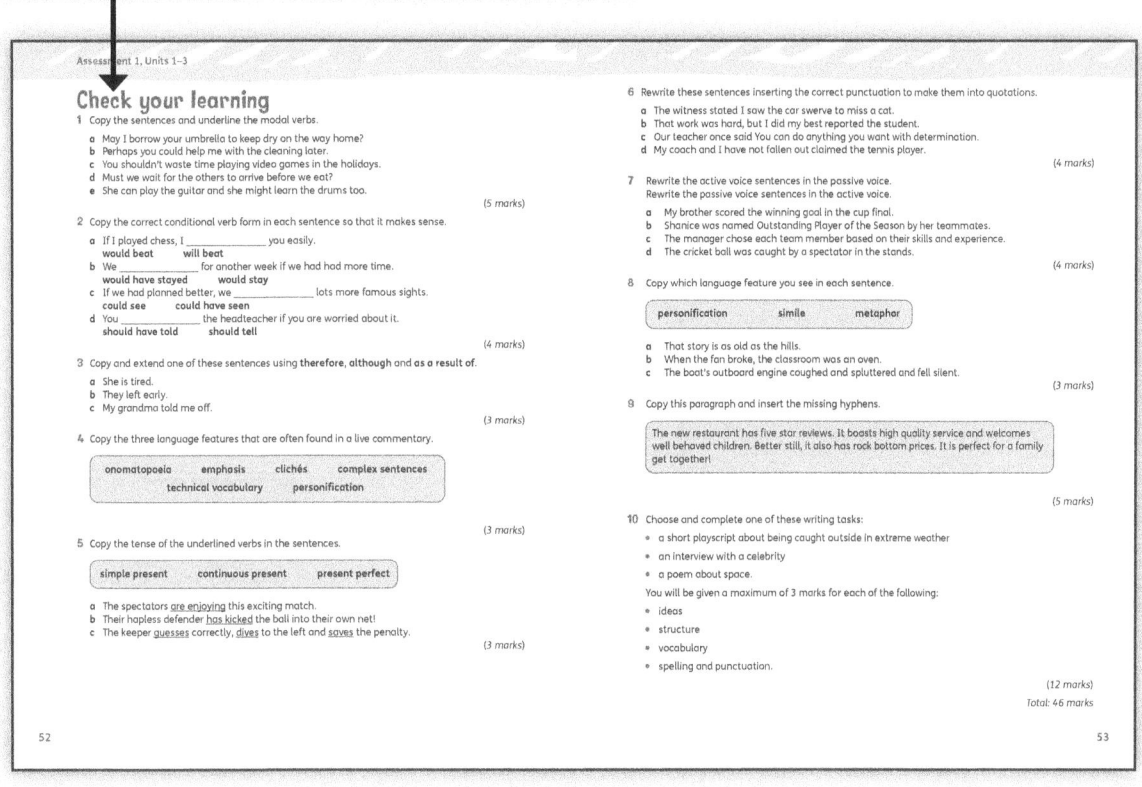

Check your learning

1 Copy the sentences and underline the modal verbs.

 a May I borrow your umbrella to keep dry on the way home?
 b Perhaps you could help me with the cleaning later.
 c You shouldn't waste time playing video games in the holidays.
 d Must we wait for the others to arrive before we eat?
 e She can play the guitar and she might learn the drums too.

(5 marks)

2 Copy the correct conditional verb form in each sentence so that it makes sense.

 a If I played chess, I _____ you easily.
    would beat   will beat
 b We _____ for another week if we had had more time.
    would have stayed   would stay
 c If we had planned better, we _____ lots of famous sights.
    could see   could have seen
 d You _____ the headteacher if you are worried about it.
    should have told   should tell

(4 marks)

3 Copy and extend one of these sentences using **therefore, although** and **as a result of.**

 a She is tired.
 b They left early.
 c My grandma told me off.

(3 marks)

4 Copy the three language features that are often found in a live commentary.

> onomatopoeia   emphasis   clichés   complex sentences
> technical vocabulary   personification

(3 marks)

5 Copy the tense of the underlined verbs in the sentences.

> simple present   continuous present   present perfect

 a The spectators <u>are enjoying</u> this exciting match.
 b Their hapless defender <u>has kicked</u> the ball into their own net!
 c The keeper <u>guesses</u> correctly, <u>dives</u> to the left and <u>saves</u> the penalty.

(3 marks)

6 Rewrite these sentences inserting the correct punctuation to make them into quotations.

 a The witness stated I saw the car swerve to miss a cat.
 b That work was hard, but I did my best reported the student.
 c Our teacher once said You can do anything you want with determination.
 d My coach and I have not fallen out claimed the tennis player.

(4 marks)

7 Rewrite the active voice sentences in the passive voice.
   Rewrite the passive voice sentences in the active voice.

 a My brother scored the winning goal in the cup final.
 b Shanice was named Outstanding Player of the Season by her teammates.
 c The manager chose each team member based on their skills and experience.
 d The cricket ball was caught by a spectator in the stands.

(4 marks)

8 Copy which language feature you see in each sentence.

> personification   simile   metaphor

 a That story is as old as the hills.
 b When the fan broke, the classroom was an oven.
 c The boat's outboard engine coughed and spluttered and fell silent.

(3 marks)

9 Copy this paragraph and insert the missing hyphens.

> The new restaurant has five star reviews. It boasts high quality service and welcomes well behaved children. Better still, it also has rock bottom prices. It is perfect for a family get together!

(5 marks)

10 Choose and complete one of these writing tasks:

 • a short playscript about being caught outside in extreme weather
 • an interview with a celebrity
 • a poem about space.

 You will be given a maximum of 3 marks for each of the following:

 • ideas
 • structure
 • vocabulary
 • spelling and punctuation.

(12 marks)

Total: 46 marks

52

53

How to use the Workbook

The Workbook is designed for independent study. Students can work on it in the classroom or at home. The Workbook consolidates, and in some cases extends, the learning objectives covered in the Student Book by providing additional practice, and applying the same skills to different texts. Because the Workbook is for students to work through independently, it covers the skills of reading, writing and language only.

Page reference
This tells you which page the activities relate to in the Student Book.

Language
These mirror the Language sections in the Student Book. Sometimes different examples are given, linked to the different texts in the Workbook, to show the language in context.

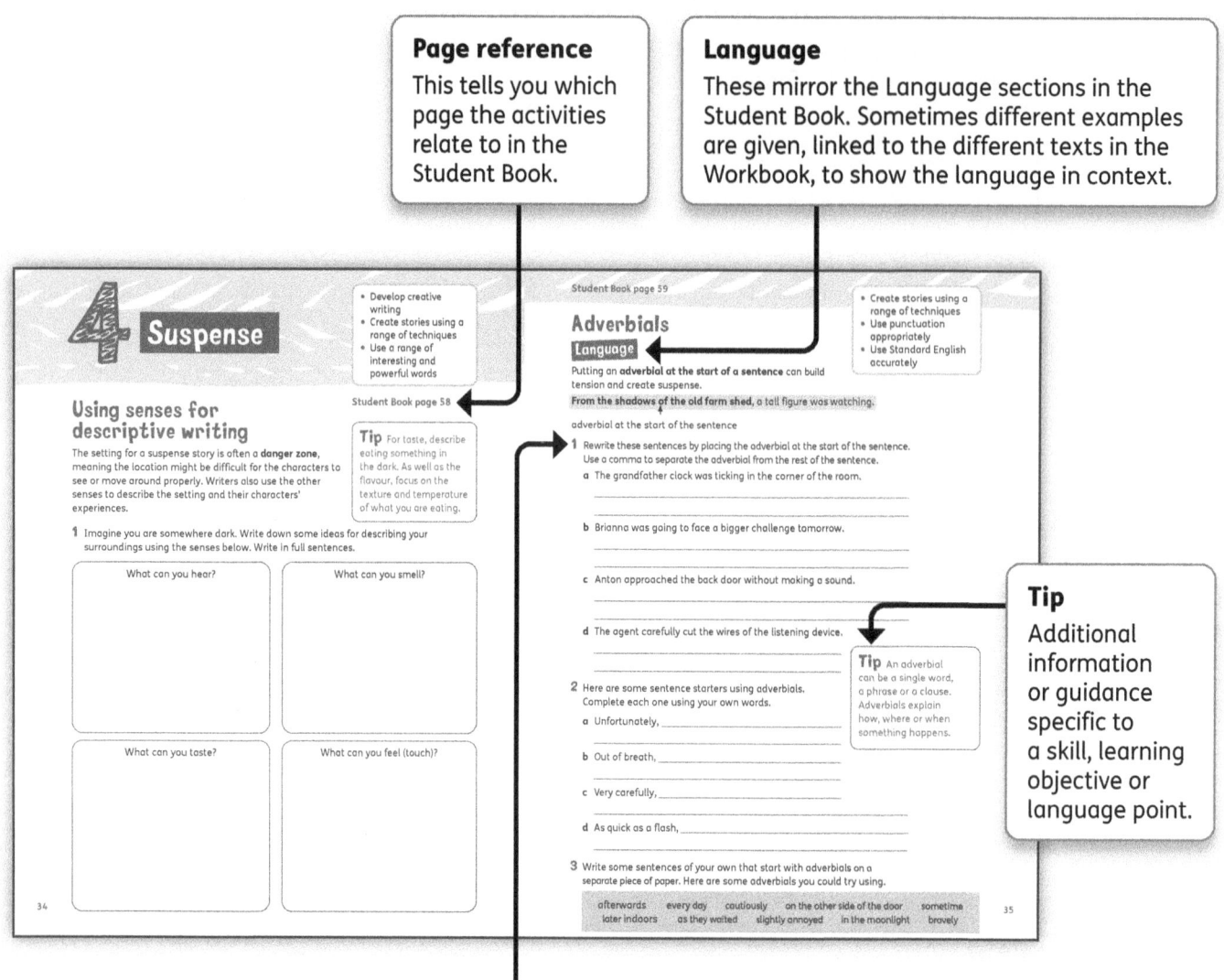

Tip
Additional information or guidance specific to a skill, learning objective or language point.

Activity
The activities in the Workbook provide more practice of the skills covered in the Student Book. The activities are differentiated so that they become progressively more challenging. For example, the first language practice activity might be identifying the form only, the second might be choosing the correct form, and the third might be producing the form correctly in the right context. You can further differentiate the Workbook activities by asking some students to complete more activities than others on a particular point, or by allowing some students to complete as many as they like of the activities linked to a particular lesson or unit. Examples are sometimes given to provide support for students when completing the activities.

Stretch activities

These activities take students beyond the learning objective. In the Workbook they are designed to be completed individually, but they can be completed in pairs in a classroom setting.

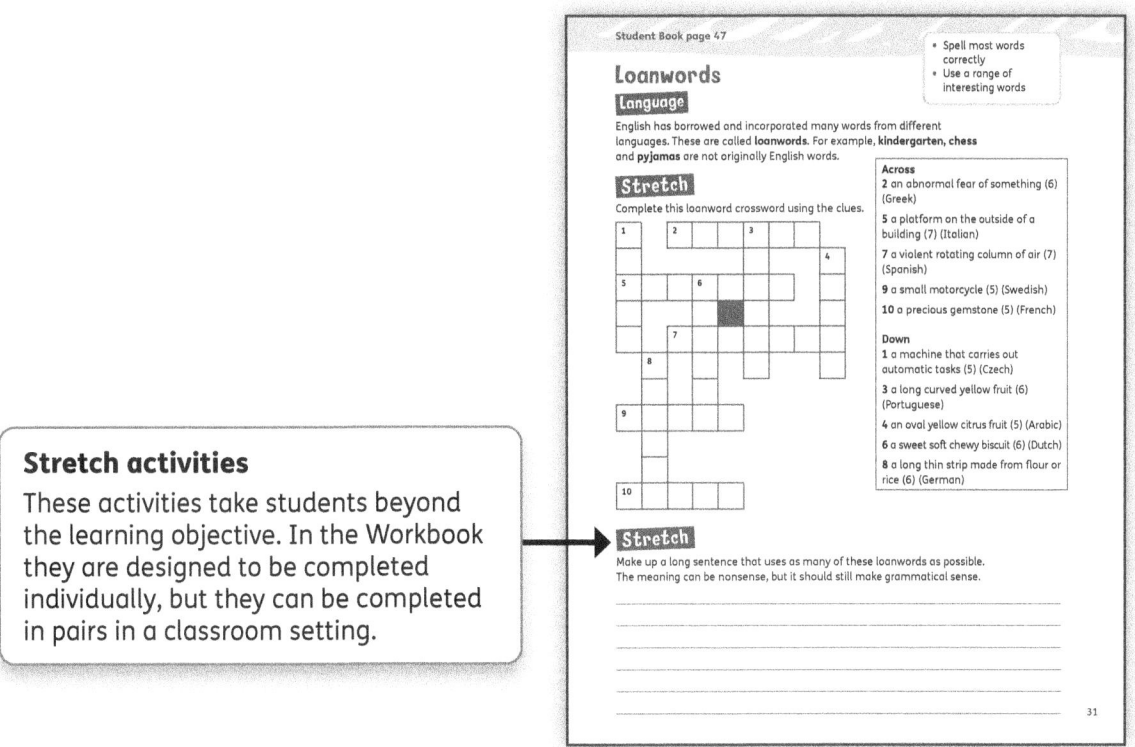

Loanwords

Language

- Spell most words correctly
- Use a range of interesting words

English has borrowed and incorporated many words from different languages. These are called **loanwords**. For example, **kindergarten, chess** and **pyjamas** are not originally English words.

Stretch

Complete this loanword crossword using the clues.

Across
2 an abnormal fear of something (6) (Greek)
5 a platform on the outside of a building (7) (Italian)
7 a violent rotating column of air (7) (Spanish)
9 a small motorcycle (5) (Swedish)
10 a precious gemstone (5) (French)

Down
1 a machine that carries out automatic tasks (5) (Czech)
3 a long curved yellow fruit (6) (Portuguese)
4 an oval yellow citrus fruit (5) (Arabic)
6 a sweet soft chewy biscuit (6) (Dutch)
8 a long thin strip made from flour or rice (6) (German)

Stretch

Make up a long sentence that uses as many of these loanwords as possible. The meaning can be nonsense, but it should still make grammatical sense.

31

Workbook checklist

Students assess how well they have achieved the unit learning objectives. This gives you valuable formative assessment feedback and allows you to adjust the learning plan to support those who are still working towards some objectives.

The Reflection questions also give you valuable formative assessment feedback, and help students to take ownership of their learning by deciding what they would like more of, and which skills they need to develop further.

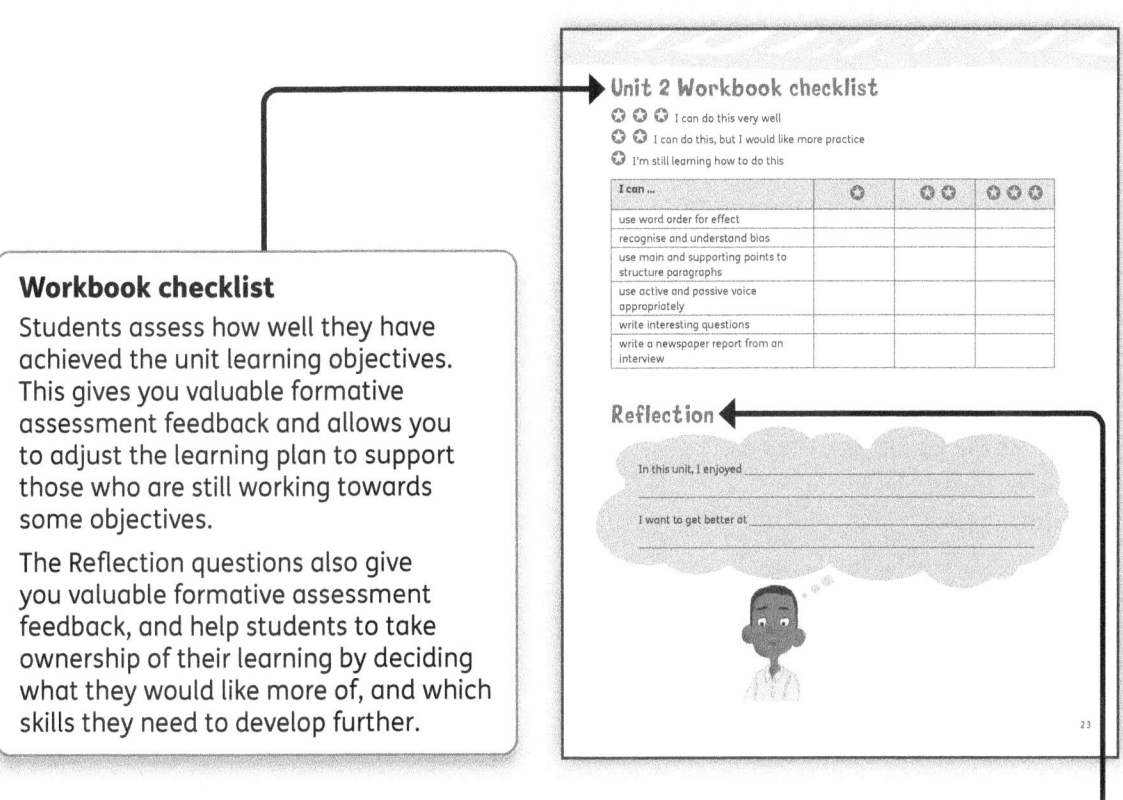

Unit 2 Workbook checklist

✪ ✪ ✪ I can do this very well
✪ ✪ I can do this, but I would like more practice
✪ I'm still learning how to do this

I can ...	✪	✪✪	✪✪✪
use word order for effect			
recognise and understand bias			
use main and supporting points to structure paragraphs			
use active and passive voice appropriately			
write interesting questions			
write a newspaper report from an interview			

Reflection

In this unit, I enjoyed _____

I want to get better at _____

23

Reflection

Students reflect on their own learning at the end of every unit. This can increase their motivation as they think about what they enjoyed and did well, and you can gain valuable, at-a-glance information about their progress.

How to use this Teacher's Guide

The Teacher's Guide gives you valuable help with lesson planning. It includes notes on activities and language to provide extra guidance which helps you make the most of the Student Book activities with your students. It includes extra teaching ideas, classroom management tips and differentiation ideas to support lower-level students and stretch higher achievers. If you read the notes on each unit before you start to teach the unit, you can plan your lessons to incorporate the extra ideas.

Notes on activities are given where they are felt to be of value, so some pages do not have additional notes, where the activities are felt to be straightforward and self-explanatory, or are similar to previous activities. This prevents repetition in the notes. For Language sections, possible pitfalls or areas of common misunderstanding are included where relevant.

The Teacher's Guide provides guidance on conducting the projects and assessments, and gives answers for the assessments and for Workbook activities. It does not provide answers to Student Book activities, since these should be self-explanatory and easy to find as you are working through the activities with students.

The Teacher's Guide also includes the transcripts of the audio texts.

Wellbeing

Let's Leap! is designed with wellbeing at the heart of the curriculum. Ways to develop students' wellbeing are embedded in the learning throughout. Students develop wellbeing skills and understanding while achieving the learning objectives in the programme of study. Many unit topics focus specifically on different aspects of wellbeing.

There are six series characters who students will meet all the way through the series (and follow their growth and development). They have been created to represent people from a range of socio-cultural and ethnic backgrounds across the Caribbean. They are:

- Aiden, who is interested in nature
- Latoya, who is athletic
- Kwame, who loves music and singing
- Priya, who loves music, dancing and baking
- Omar, who is kind, helpful and likes to make things
- Maya, who is a hardworking budding gymnast.

Students will read stories about each of these characters, and the characters will ask questions that help students with their learning. The texts are written to show the characters in different situations that the students may encounter in their lives, and the activities encourage them to empathise with the characters in the texts, while developing their reading and literary analysis skills. For example, students are encouraged to consider how they would feel in a similar situation, and what they would do, or what they think the character should do, next. Thus the development of wellbeing skills is inseparable from the development of the learning objectives.

The main areas of wellbeing developed in the series include physical wellbeing, emotional and psychological wellbeing, social wellbeing and care for others. For example, units focusing on physical wellbeing include healthy eating, personal hygiene, physical fitness, the need for sleep. Units that develop emotional and psychological wellbeing include overcoming fears, developing resilience, building self-confidence, recognising your talents. Social wellbeing and care for others is developed in topics such as being kind, how to be a good friend, being kind to older community members, taking care of or helping animals, making good decisions in different situations.

The strong focus on students' speaking and listening in the classroom gives you ample opportunity to be aware of any potential wellbeing issues for individual students as they share their ideas and experiences with a partner. The Let's talk activities in many of the units encourage them to share personal experiences in a safe situation with a partner. This enables you to find out more, and to provide intervention or support as appropriate.

The overall aim of developing wellbeing skills through the course is to teach students how to love: to develop love of self, love of others, love of nature and other living things, love of their environment, home and culture. It is hoped that students will also develop a love of learning that will enable them to achieve their full potential in the Primary Arts curriculum, to be well prepared for their later education, and to lead fulfilling and successful lives.

Extra support

A wealth of additional supplementary resources for *Let's Leap!* exist in digital format. Visit the course companion site: https://www.oxfordprimary.com/letsleappla to access downloadable glossaries, irregular verb tables, as well as writing templates and planners. On this site you will also find a levels-matching grid explaining how *Let's Leap!* resources correlate to your primary school structure, wherever you are across the Caribbean, plus detailed biographies for all of the series characters.

Digital (interactive) editions of the Student Books are available as part of the course, which include the audio files for the speaking and listening tasks. These books have offline capability and are fully in line with Web Content Accessibility Guidelines (WCAG) in terms of fonts, images and colour vision deficiency. To access the Digital Student Book, please follow the instructions on the inside front cover of this Teacher's Guide.

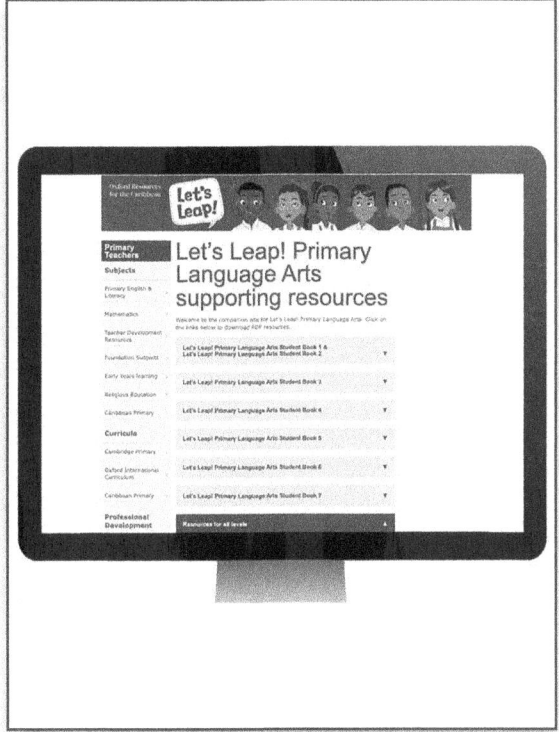

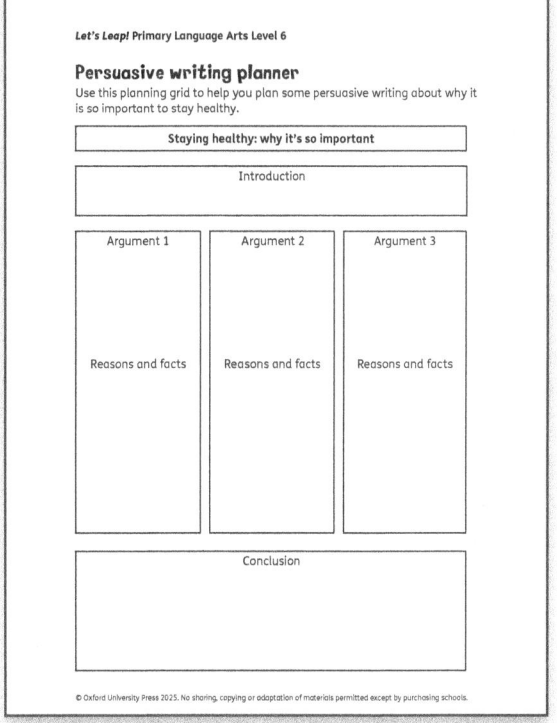

Let's Leap! programme of study for Level 7

7SL Speaking and listening

Making yourself understood (speaking)

1. Speak with confidence, fluency and accurate pronunciation on a wide range of familiar and unfamiliar topics
2. Express ideas, opinions and feelings with increasing detail and clarity, justifying own viewpoint and linking it to others' viewpoints
3. Describe a range of people, places and objects and events in detail using a range of mainly accurate language, choosing interesting language
4. Speak freely, fluently and confidently and at increasing length in Creole and Standard English
5. Use Creole and different registers of Standard English appropriately in a wide range of different contexts to express a wide range of feelings and ideas

Showing understanding (listening)

6. Understand explicit and implicit meaning and details in a range of longer and increasingly complex talk

Performance

7. Read aloud fluently and confidently, with appropriate expression, in a wide range of longer texts
8. Plan, write and act a scene from life or fiction, acting convincingly
9. Plan and deliver a presentation, adapting the content and language to the audience

Group work and discussions

10. Listen and respond appropriately in a wide range of speaking activities
11. Ask and answer a wide range of questions asking for detailed information and seeking clarification
12. Take turns when speaking in a range of longer, more complex exchanges, keeping the conversation going, and concluding it effectively
13. Take part in group discussions and problem-solving activities and extended projects, working together to achieve an outcome

7R Reading

Reading for understanding

1. Ask and answer a range of questions about longer texts and summarise the main and supporting points
2. Understand the purpose of a wide range of different texts, including different genres of fiction
3. Understand the purpose of different parts of a text in a wide range of texts, including genres of fiction

Reading critically/interpreting texts (including media and literary texts)

4. Explore characters' feelings, personalities and motivations in increasing detail, referring to the text and relating to own experience or other reading
5. Explore the language in a wide range of longer Creole and Standard English texts, e.g. poems, stories, age-appropriate novels and non-fiction texts
6. Explore a range of literary features and discuss writers' intentions, beginning to give support from the text
7. Talk about stories and poems they like in detail and give reasons, referring to the text

Word reading

8. Read age-appropriate texts fluently and with understanding

7W Writing

Word writing

1. Spell most words correctly and proofread own and others' work for accuracy
2. Develop strategies including using known spelling patterns to predict spelling of new words

Creation of texts

3. Plan and develop creative writing in a range of different genres of fiction, non-fiction and types of poem, using the most appropriate planning method
4. Create stories using a range of techniques, e.g. different points of view, creating suspense
5. Write a range of non-fiction text types for different audiences and purposes using appropriate features and adapting language for different audiences
6. Write a range of literary texts of increasing length, e.g. stories, poems and scripts using literary devices studied so far for effect
7. Evaluate own and others' writing, suggesting improvements including making the writing more powerful and evaluating literary devices

Presentation/organisation (including media and literary texts)

8. Write legibly and with appropriate speed and fluency
9. Write longer texts, grouping ideas in paragraphs and with an opening and a conclusion
10. Use appropriate layout when writing a wide range of longer texts, e.g. stories, poems, information texts, presentations, scripts
11. Use a wide range of punctuation appropriately

7L Language

Vocabulary

1. Use a wide range of language forms appropriately
2. Use a wide range of interesting and powerful new words
3. Recognise and use a wide range of synonyms and antonyms
4. Use a wide range of prefixes and suffixes with verbs, nouns, adjectives and adverbs
5. Use knowledge of word formation to understand and use new words

Language structure

6. Use a range of structural features for effect, e.g. dramatic effect, suspense
7. Use Standard English accurately and at increasing length for a range of topics, purposes and audiences

Programme of study: Learning outcomes

Student Book 7 Learning outcomes

Unit	Topic	Texts	Speaking and listening	Reading	Writing
1	Beyond Earth	Non-fiction: Travelling through space, Features of a playscript Fiction: *Red Horizon*	7SL1 7SL2 7SL3 7SL4 7SL5 7SL7 7SL8 7SL10 7SL11 7SL12 7SL13	7R1 7R3 7R4 7R6 7R8	7W3 7W4 7W6 7W7 7W10 7W11
2	Sports	Listening: Live commentaries Non-fiction: Newspaper reports, Features of a newspaper report	7SL1 7SL2 7SL3 7SL4 7SL5 7SL6 7SL8 7SL9 7SL10 7SL11 7SL12 7SL13	7R1 7R2 7R3 7R4 7R5 7R6 7R8 Understanding bias	7W3 7W5 7W6 7W7 7W9 7W11
3	Mother Nature	Poetry: Hurricane, Stormman, Bush fire, Frost, Fog	7SL1 7SL2 7SL3 7SL4 7SL5 7SL7 7SL9 7SL10 7SL11 7SL12 7SL13	7R1 7R5 7R6 7R7	7W1 7W3 7W6 7W7 7W10 7W11
4	Suspense	Listening: *A night in the jungle* Fiction: *In the dark*	7SL1 7SL2 7SL3 7SL4 7SL5 7SL8 7SL12 7SL13	7R1 7R2 7R3 7R4 7R6 7R7 7R8	7W1 7W3 7W4 7W6 7W7 7W9 7W10 7W11
5	Making a difference	Non-fiction: Q&A with a climate student, Persuasive writing, Facts and opinions, Taking action for the environment	7SL1 7SL2 7SL3 7SL4 7SL5 7SL7 7SL9 7SL11 7SL12 7SL13	7R1 7R2 7R3 7R5 7R8	7W2 7W3 7W5 7W7 7W8 7W10
6	Creating characters	Fiction: Character descriptions and backstories, Show, don't tell, What other characters think, Challenging your character	7SL1 7SL2 7SL3 7SL4 7SL5 7SL6 7SL10 7SL11 7SL12 7SL13	7R1 7R4 7R5 7R8	7W1 7W3 7W4 7W5 7W7 7W8 7W9
7	Exploring food	Fiction: *The new school menu* Non-fiction: Balanced arguments Listening: *New food*	7SL1 7SL2 7SL3 7SL4 7SL5 7SL7 7SL9 7SL10 7SL11 7SL12 7SL13	7R1 7R3 7R4 7R5	7W1 7W2 7W5 7W7 7W9 7W11
8	Moving on	Non-fiction: Looking back and looking forward Poetry: Childhood Tracks, The Yacht, Bittersweet Non-fiction: A letter to my future self	7SL1 7SL2 7SL3 7SL4 7SL5 7SL7 7SL11 7SL12 7SL13	7R1 7R4 7R5 7R6 7R7 7R8	7W1 7W2 7W3 7W5 7W6 7W7 7W8 7W10 7W11
9	Preparing for tests	Non-fiction: Let's prepare for a test, Study tips	N/A	N/A	N/A

Language structure and vocabulary	Projects
7L1 7L6 7L7 Modal verbs of possibility and permission Extending sentences Modal verbs of ability, obligation and advice Conditional sentences	Project 1: Performance Perform *Red Horizon* using the playscript and writing additional scenes Project 2: Writing Review of another group's version of *Red Horizon*
7L1 7L6 7L7 Emphasis and bias Active and passive voices Open and closed questions	Project 1: Performance Role-play live commentary for a live sports event Project 2: Writing Fact file on sport as poster, booklet or on-screen presentation
7L1 7L2 7L3 7L5 Figurative language Word choice Punctuation: Hyphens Building vocabulary Loanwords	Project 1: Performance Perform own Mother Nature poems Project 2: Writing Group poem
7L1 7L2 7L6 Descriptive writing Adverbials Building tension and creating suspense Using ellipses and single dashes for suspense	Project 1: Writing Suspense playscript Project 2: Performance Suspense play
7L1 7L4 7L5 Making adjectives from nouns Less common prefixes Features of a persuasive text Purpose, form, audience and tone Facts and opinions Linking ideas using connectives Personal and impersonal tones	Project 1: Writing Fact file Project 2: Performance Fact file and materials presentation, Q&A, feedback survey
7L2 7L3 7L7 Identifying characteristics Participle adjectives Describing appearance Describing personality Direct speech	Project 1: Performance 'Guess Who' game Project 2: Writing Character creation
7L1 7L6 7L7 Phrasal verbs Silent letters and unstressed vowels Impersonal voice and quantifiers Connectives in balanced arguments Colons and semi-colons	Project 1: Writing Food and dishes fact file Project 2: Performance Debate
7L1 7L7 Oxymorons Symbolism Punctuating a letter Commas (revision) Types of compound words	Project 1: Performance School memories poems Project 2: Writing Letter to the youngest students in school
N/A	N/A

Workbook 7 Learning outcomes

Unit	Topic	Texts	Reading	Writing
1	Beyond Earth	Non-fiction: Caribbean astronauts (report)	7R1 7R5 7R6 7R8	7W3 7W4 7W5 7W6 7W8 Explanation text Playscript
2	Sports	Non-fiction: Live commentary (transcript) Non-fiction: A star athlete retires (newspaper report)	7R1 7R3 7R4 7R5 7R8	7W3 7W5 7W11 Commentary Newspaper report
3	Mother Nature	Poetry: The Monster in the Mountain	7R1 7R3 7R7 7R8	7W1 7W3 7W4 7W6 7W11 Story opening Poem
4	Suspense	Fiction: The Mirror Man (short story)	7R1 7R3 7R6 7R8	7W3 7W4 7W6 7W9 7W11 Descriptive text Suspense story
5	Making a difference	Non-fiction: Persuasive writing (letter)	7R1 7R2 7R3 7R5 7R6 7R8	7W2 7W3 7W5 7W10 Non-fiction text Persuasive letter
6	Creating characters	Fiction: Reading for explicit and implicit information Fiction: What other characters think	7R1 7R3 7R4 7R6 7R8	7W3 7W4 7W11 Character descriptions Story
7	Exploring food	Non-fiction: Should fast food have an age restriction? (balanced argument)	7R1 7R3 7R5 7R6 7R8	7W2 7W3 7W5 7W8 7W10 7W11 Food experience Balanced argument
8	Moving on	N/A	N/A	7W2 7W3 7W5 7W6 7W8 7W11 A sensory memory Recount from school School memories poem Aspirations
9	Preparing for tests	Non-fiction: Helping your child prepare for a test Non-fiction: Party invitation Poetry: Sweet and Low	N/A	N/A

Language structure and vocabulary
7L1 7L2 7L5 7L7 Modal verbs of possibility and permission Extending sentences Features of a playscript Modal verbs of ability, obligation and advice Conditional sentences
7L1 7L6 7L7 Emphasis and bias Quotations Active and passive voices
7L1 7L2 7L3 Personification Word choice and hyphens Similes Metaphors Loanwords
7L1 7L2 7L6 7L7 Adverbials Building tension with promise sentences and questions Creating more suspense Using ellipses and single dashes for suspense
7L1 7L4 7L5 7L6 7L7 Making adjectives from nouns Less common prefixes Features of a persuasive text Purpose, form, audience and tone Facts and opinions
7L2 7L3 7L4 7L7 Participle adjectives Describing appearance and personality Writing a backstory Reading for explicit and implicit information Direct speech
7L1 7L2 7L6 7L7 Phrasal verbs Silent letters and unstressed vowels Impersonal voice and quantifiers Connectives in balanced arguments Colons and semi-colons
7L1 7L6 7L7 Oxymorons A review of literary devices Punctuating a letter Types of compound words
N/A

1 Beyond Earth

Unit opener
page 4

Learning objectives

7SL1 Speak with confidence, fluency and accurate pronunciation on a wide range of familiar and unfamiliar topics

7SL2 Express ideas, opinions and feelings with increasing detail and clarity, justifying own viewpoint and linking it to others' viewpoints

7SL3 Describe a range of people, places and objects and events in detail using a range of mainly accurate language, choosing interesting language

7SL4 Speak freely, fluently and confidently and at increasing length in Creole and Standard English

7SL5 Use Creole and different registers of Standard English appropriately in a wide range of different contexts to express a wide range of feelings and ideas

7SL12 Take turns when speaking in a range of longer, more complex exchanges, keeping the conversation going, and concluding it effectively

Images and Let's talk (see introduction on page x)

- Use the pictures and the Let's talk questions as a way to gauge students' prior knowledge on the topic, to determine how much detail you can go into, or whether further information is needed to introduce the topic.
- Write *Beyond* on the board. Encourage volunteers to explain what this means and elicit some examples. Have students open their Student Books and read the unit's title aloud. Encourage students to say what this means and connect it with the pictures.
- Have pairs answer the questions. Remind students to take turns politely. Check as a class. Additionally, you can ask students to research space expeditions and share their findings next lesson.

Reading: Travelling through space
page 5

Learning objective

7R8 Read age-appropriate texts fluently and with understanding

Let's read (see introduction on page xi)

- Focus on the picture and have volunteers describe it. Encourage them to say who this is, what they are doing, what we can see in the background, what is reflected on the helmet, and so on.
- Tell students they are about to read an article. Elicit if this is fiction or non-fiction, its purpose and some features. Take notes and keep them to display the next lesson.
- Set up a jigsaw reading. Divide the class into groups of four and have each member read one paragraph. Then ask them to share what their text is about. Ask volunteers to mention information they didn't know.
- If time allows, have students read the text again on their own. Have them note down any vocabulary they do not know. Ask them to share the words in their group and try to explain their meaning. If nobody knows what a word means, encourage them to check in a dictionary.

Reading and speaking: Travelling through space (continued)
page 6

Learning objectives

7R1 Ask and answer a range of questions about longer texts and summarise the main and supporting points

7R8 Read age-appropriate texts fluently and with understanding

Let's read

- Have pairs try to answer the Let's talk questions before reading the second part of the article. This will help them remember what they learned in the previous lesson and speculate about the contents of today's section.
- Tell students to read the text and check if their answers were correct.

Activity (see introduction on page x)

- Display the notes about the article features you took the previous lesson. Check them against the article. Have small groups discuss question 1.

Speaking and listening: Would you volunteer to go to space? page 7

Learning objectives

7SL1 Speak with confidence, fluency and accurate pronunciation on a wide range of familiar and unfamiliar topics

7SL2 Express ideas, opinions and feelings with increasing detail and clarity, justifying own viewpoint and linking it to others' viewpoints

7SL10 Listen and respond appropriately in a wide range of speaking activities

7SL11 Ask and answer a wide range of questions asking for detailed information and seeking clarification

7SL12 Take turns when speaking in a range of longer, more complex exchanges, keeping the conversation going, and concluding it effectively

7SL13 Take part in group discussions and problem-solving activities and extended projects, working together to achieve an outcome

Activity

- Active listening requires practice. Before you start the activity, go through the Active listening guidelines and model each with a volunteer. Alternatively, it may be more memorable to model the opposite of each suggestion first so that students realise what bad practices look like. For example, have a conversation with a volunteer and look away. Then ask the volunteer how they felt and what would be a better way of having the conversation so that students suggest we should face people when speaking.
- You can make this activity teacher-led and focus on listening skills with limited opportunity for Q&A and debate. Maintain strict control of any discussion as the emphasis is on listening to a range of views and reflection rather than debate. Students can use a 'speaking object', such as an eraser, that signals the only person allowed to speak is whoever is holding the object. Be aware of the timing of the 'reflection moments' to allow students to take a break from listening to think and then to refocus on active listening. Emphasise that students are free to change their minds or not and to embrace being open-minded.

Language: Modal verbs of possibility and permission page 8

Learning objectives

7W7 Evaluate own and others' writing, suggesting improvements including making the writing more powerful and evaluating literary devices

7L1 Use a wide range of language forms appropriately

7L7 Use Standard English accurately and at increasing length for a range of topics, purposes and audiences

Activity

- Activate students' prior knowledge by listing down the modals on the board (can, could, may, might). Draw a two-column table with the headings *Permission* and *Possibility*. Have pairs classify the modals; remind them some can go in both columns. Ask them to check their answers against the Student Book table.
- Lead and model the activity. Decide on which forms to teach, for example, whether to use *cannot*, *can't* or both; whether to use *might not* or the contraction *mightn't*.

Stretch (see introduction on page xi)

- Students may have used *can* as ability in the previous activity, which would open the discussion about other concepts.
- If necessary, help students recognise that *can* is a modal of ability. Say *I can swim well* and ask if this is permission or possibility; lead them to say the sentence expresses ability. This will be covered in more detail on page 14.

Language: Extending sentences page 9

Learning objective

7L6 Use a range of structural features for effect, e.g. dramatic effect, suspense

Activity

- You can extend the activity for small groups. Each group should have a soft ball or any object they can toss without hurting anyone. The first volunteer of each group says a short sentence and tosses the ball to another group member, who should extend it. Then they repeat the process for the next student to keep extending the sentence. The challenge is to create the longest sentence they can make up. The group with the longest sentence wins the game.

Reading: Red Horizon   page 10

Learning objectives

7SL7 Read aloud fluently and confidently, with appropriate expression, in a wide range of longer texts

7R4 Explore characters' feelings, personalities and motivations in increasing detail, referring to the text and relating to own experience or other reading

Let's read

- Allow students to read the script on their own. Draw their attention to the information in italics and in brackets and elicit what these words are for. Check their answers against the Tip.

Reading: Red Horizon (continued)   page 11

Learning objectives

7SL7 Read aloud fluently and confidently, with appropriate expression, in a wide range of longer texts

7SL8 Plan, write and act a scene from life or fiction, acting convincingly

7R4 Explore characters' feelings, personalities and motivations in increasing detail, referring to the text and relating to own experience or other reading

Activity

- Encourage students to add body language to their performance.
- Ask volunteer pairs to perform one section for the rest of the class. Optionally, you or another student could read the stage directions.

Reading: A cliffhanger   page 12

Learning objectives

7SL2 Express ideas, opinions and feelings with increasing detail and clarity, justifying own viewpoint and linking it to others' viewpoints

7SL7 Read aloud fluently and confidently, with appropriate expression, in a wide range of longer texts

7SL8 Plan, write and act a scene from life or fiction, acting convincingly

7W11 Use a wide range of punctuation appropriately

Activity

- Alternatively, you can divide the class into groups of four, making sure students work with partners they haven't worked with recently. Tell them to take turns playing different roles: stage director, Denzil,

Ruby and Sachin. The stage director can suggest ways for the actors to improve their performance, either using their voice or adding body language.

Reading and writing: Features of a playscript   page 13

Learning objectives

7R3 Understand the purpose of different parts of a text in a wide range of texts, including genres of fiction

7R6 Explore a range of literary features and discuss writers' intentions, beginning to give support from the text

7W7 Evaluate own and others' writing, suggesting improvements including making the writing more powerful and evaluating literary devices

Let's read

- Ask students to read the script individually, not paying attention to the labels. Ask some comprehension questions, for example: *Where is this happening? What's wrong with Kwame? Why isn't Kwame happy with Tiyana?*
- Have groups of three perform the script and then direct students' attention to the labelled features. Invite a student to explain how it helps the actors to perform better.
- Divide the class into pairs and tell them to analyse five features each and share their analysis with partners. Check answers as a class.

Language: Modal verbs of ability, obligation and advice   page 14

Learning objectives

7W7 Evaluate own and others' writing, suggesting improvements including making the writing more powerful and evaluating literary devices

7L1 Use a wide range of language forms appropriately

7L7 Use Standard English accurately and at increasing length for a range of topics, purposes and audiences

Language (see introduction on page xi)

- Activate students' prior knowledge and ask why modal verbs are also called helpful verbs. Elicit some examples and encourage volunteers to say what they are expressing. For example: *I might go to the cinema this weekend – possibility*. Elicit modal verbs for possibility and permission.
- Write the headings *Advice, Obligation* and *Ability* on the board. Have small groups write as many modal verbs for each category as they can. Tell them to write an example for each. Remind them that modal verbs

can be used in the past, present and future tenses, as well as in the negative. Check as a class and refer to the Student Book information as necessary.

Language: Conditional sentences
page 15

Learning objectives
7L1 Use a wide range of language forms appropriately

7L7 Use Standard English accurately and at increasing length for a range of topics, purposes and audiences

Activity
- Monitor students' work and assess if more controlled or freer practice is needed. You may want to divide the class into groups according to their abilities and assign extra help accordingly. For example, elicit verbs and write on the board the ones that can be easily used as prompts in conditional sentences. For controlled practice: students choose a number 1–3 and make up the corresponding first, second or third conditional. For semi-controlled practice: each student adapts the same words and makes first, second and third conditional sentences. For freer practice: assign each group a 1–6 spinner and write this code on the board: *1 or 4 = first, 2 or 5 = second, 3 or 6 = third*. Each student spins a number and makes up the corresponding conditional.

Speaking and Listening: What happens next?
page 16

Learning objectives
7SL2 Express ideas, opinions and feelings with increasing detail and clarity, justifying own viewpoint and linking it to others' viewpoints

7SL4 Speak freely, fluently and confidently and at increasing length in Creole and Standard English

7SL10 Listen and respond appropriately in a wide range of speaking activities

7SL12 Take turns when speaking in a range of longer, more complex exchanges, keeping the conversation going, and concluding it effectively

7SL13 Take part in group discussions and problem-solving activities and extended projects, working together to achieve an outcome

Let's read
- Divide the class into groups of three and ask them to choose a character to read their lines (Ruby, Sachin or Denzil). Tell them to keep this character for the interview of Activity question 2.

Activity
- Read the Group discussion rules before setting groups to work on question 3. It may be a good idea to model the chairperson's role with a small group. Show how to invite people to speak one by one, thank them for their contribution and how to remind people not to interrupt, and so on.
- Stress the authority of the chairperson by asking them to feed back after the discussion on how well their group interacted and followed the discussion rules.

Writing: Playscript writing
page 17

Learning objectives
7W3 Plan and develop creative writing in a range of different genres of fiction, non-fiction and types of poem, using the most appropriate planning method

7W4 Create stories using a range of techniques, e.g. different points of view, creating suspense

7W7 Evaluate own and others' writing, suggesting improvements including making the writing more powerful and evaluating literary devices

7W10 Use appropriate layout when writing a wide range of longer texts, e.g. stories, poems, information texts, presentations, scripts

7W11 Use a wide range of punctuation appropriately

Activity
- Students can use the Playscript planner on Workbook page 12 to help them organise their ideas (this is also on page 59 of this Teacher's Guide).
- You may want to reinforce the idea of self-correction by allowing students to correct their own first draft. Remind them to check vocabulary, grammar, spelling and punctuation when they finish their playscript. Then ask them to go through the Playscript checklist and underline any aspects that can be improved.
- Allow them to write a second draft for a partner to check.
- Remind students of the importance of respectful and useful feedback. Encourage them to read the feedback and make sure they understand it. They can ask the author to clarify if necessary. Explain that not all feedback should be followed. This is an opinion that can help them shape their work better but the last word is theirs. Monitor and help if necessary.

Project 1: Performance

Learning objectives

7SL8 Plan, write and act a scene from life or fiction, acting convincingly

7SL12 Take turns when speaking in a range of longer, more complex exchanges, keeping the conversation going, and concluding it effectively

7SL13 Take part in group discussions and problem-solving activities and extended projects, working together to achieve an outcome

7W6 Write a range of literary texts of increasing length, e.g. stories, poems and scripts using literary devices studied so far for effect

7W7 Evaluate own and others' writing, suggesting improvements including making the writing more powerful and evaluating literary devices

Project guidance (see introduction on page xii)

- If time allows, both projects can be completed in one session or in several sessions throughout the unit. You may prefer to choose one project for students to complete. Alternatively, you may wish to give students the choice of which project they would like to complete.
- If some students are working more than other group members, you can reassign the roles or tasks.
- Allow groups to work together to give feedback. Remind them to be respectful of everyone's work.
- At least three people are needed in a group to play the main characters. However, some students may have included one or two extra characters in the writing task; some juggling of groups may be necessary. Ensure that all group members get a speaking part, however small.
- It is likely that students request to use and/or make props for Step 5. Decide whether this will benefit the project as students can potentially focus more on prop preparation than the performance itself.
- Consider splitting performances up over a number of sessions to allow students to appreciate each other's work without too much repetition. Ask for some immediate positive feedback to be voiced, then allow each group a few minutes to discuss and note down their reactions in more detail, before moving on to the next performance.
- You can ask students to make a special section in their notebooks for their Project reflection. Tell them to write what they can do better next time and encourage them to refer to these notes when starting a new unit project.
- Less confident students may benefit from having a checklist of features to improve their performance. You can create very simple guidelines with four or five points to bear in mind.

Project 2: Writing

Learning objectives

7SL7 Read aloud fluently and confidently, with appropriate expression, in a wide range of longer texts

7W7 Evaluate own and others' writing, suggesting improvements including making the writing more powerful and evaluating literary devices

Project guidance

- Ask students to research the features of a review. Assess how much more input is required about the format or features and how much scaffolding is required, for example, the use of a template.
- Encourage group members to choose their role according to their strengths: some may be good at summarising while others are really good at spotting spelling and grammar mistakes. Monitor the groups and make sure the work distribution is fair.

Sports

Unit opener	page 20

Learning objectives

7SL1 Speak with confidence, fluency and accurate pronunciation on a wide range of familiar and unfamiliar topics

7SL2 Express ideas, opinions and feelings with increasing detail and clarity, justifying own viewpoint and linking it to others' viewpoints

7SL3 Describe a range of people, places and objects and events in detail using a range of mainly accurate language, choosing interesting language

7SL4 Speak freely, fluently and confidently and at increasing length in Creole and Standard English

7SL5 Use Creole and different registers of Standard English appropriately in a wide range of different contexts to express a wide range of feelings and ideas

7SL12 Take turns when speaking in a range of longer, more complex exchanges, keeping the conversation going, and concluding it effectively

Images and Let's talk

- Use the pictures and the Let's talk questions as a way to gauge students' prior knowledge on the topic, to determine how much detail you can go into, or whether further information is needed to introduce the topic.
- Write *Sports* on the board. Encourage volunteers to add as many names of sports using the base word to make a crossword. For example, students can write *basketball* vertically using either *s* in *sports* and then *track and field* using the *t* in *basketball*, and so on.
- Ask the class which of the sports on the board they like and or practise. Focus on the Student Book pictures and encourage students to name the sports and give details about them. Ask: *Are these individual or team sports? Do they require equipment?*
- Have pairs answer the questions. Remind students to take turns politely. Check as a class.

Listening and speaking: Live commentary: Part 1	page 21

Learning objectives

7SL5 Use Creole and different registers of Standard English appropriately in a wide range of different contexts to express a wide range of feelings and ideas

7SL6 Understand explicit and implicit meaning and details in a range of longer and increasingly complex talk

7SL11 Ask and answer a wide range of questions asking for detailed information and seeking clarification

7L6 Use a range of structural features for effect, e.g. dramatic effect, suspense

Let's listen

- Elicit some of the sports mentioned on page 20 and ask which usually have live commentaries. Give some examples to get across meaning. Draw out what a commentator does – providing live commentary – and ask students how hard or easy this job is. Encourage volunteers to say which skills commentators need to be good at their jobs.
- Assign a simple while-listening task to help students focus. For example, write down the names of the athletes mentioned (Clarke and Brown).

Activity

- Encourage students to note down the words that made them choose the sports. Try to use this practice whenever possible as it benefits students to sustain their answers whenever they are giving an opinion.

Listening: Live commentary: Part 2	page 22

Learning objectives

7SL5 Use Creole and different registers of Standard English appropriately in a wide range of different contexts to express a wide range of feelings and ideas

7SL6 Understand explicit and implicit meaning and details in a range of longer and increasingly complex talk

7SL11 Ask and answer a wide range of questions asking for detailed information and seeking clarification

7L6 Use a range of structural features for effect, e.g. dramatic effect, suspense

Let's listen

- Tell students they will hear a commentary on a cricket match. Ask students to copy onto their notebooks the words from the box of Activity question 1 before they listen to the live commentary; some students may be familiar with some of them but reassure them they do not need to know what they mean as now they are focusing on their sound.
- Ask students to listen to the track and cross out each word when they hear it mentioned.
- Only *fielder* and *delivery* are not mentioned in the commentary.

Activity

- Encourage students to use dictionaries to check any unfamiliar cricketing terms but be ready to explain if necessary.
- If you have repeated the track to check answers and some students are still unsure, you can refer to the audioscript on page 56 of the Teacher's Guide to settle any differences. You can also display the script (e.g. on-screen or typed out again) without the unit number or any reference that can give away where this was taken from.

Speaking and writing: Emphasis
page 23

Learning objectives

7SL5 Use Creole and different registers of Standard English appropriately in a wide range of different contexts to express a wide range of feelings and ideas

7L6 Use a range of structural features for effect, e.g. dramatic effect, suspense

Let's talk

- To reinforce the impact of emphasis and how it varies meaning, you can write a sentence on the board and say it aloud emphasising a different word each time. For example: *I have never seen that before! I have **never** seen that before! I have **seen** that before! I have never seen **that** before! I have never seen that **before**!* Pause after a few examples and elicit the differences in meaning.

Activity 1

- Help students to notice the inversion of subject verbs. Explain that this is done mainly in writing and makes the register formal. Tell students they can use the same adverbs with no inversion while speaking if they want to emphasise something without making it sound too formal.

Reading: Bias
page 24

Learning objectives

7R2 Understand the purpose of a wide range of different texts, including different genres of fiction

7R5 Explore the language in a wide range of longer Creole and Standard English texts, e.g. poems, stories, age-appropriate novels and non-fiction texts

Activity

- Allow your students to create biased comments on their own. They usually find the activity fun and memorable. Divide the class into pairs and tell them to choose one of the series characters. You may want to elicit information about each and write it on the board.
- Have students write as many biased sentences about their character as possible in two minutes, asking them to omit their character's name.
- Ask them to swap their sentences and classify them into opinion, statements without facts and prejudice. Encourage volunteers to read some examples for the rest of the class to guess who is being described and say which type of biased sentence it is.

Speaking and writing: Role-play
page 25

Learning objectives

7SL1 Speak with confidence, fluency and accurate pronunciation on a wide range of familiar and unfamiliar topics

7SL8 Plan, write and act a scene from life or fiction, acting convincingly

7W5 Write a range of non-fiction text types for different audiences and purposes using appropriate features and adapting language for different audiences

7L7 Use Standard English accurately and at increasing length for a range of topics, purposes and audiences

Activity 2

- You may want to reinforce the work of self-correction by allowing pairs to correct their newspaper report when they finish writing it. Tell them to check vocabulary, grammar, spelling and punctuation. Then ask them to go through the report again and underline any aspects that can be improved.
- Allow them to write a second draft for their partners to check.

Reading: Understanding bias page 26

Learning objectives

7W3 Plan and develop creative writing in a range of different genres of fiction, non-fiction and types of poem, using the most appropriate planning method

7W5 Write a range of non-fiction text types for different audiences and purposes using appropriate features and adapting language for different audiences

7W6 Write a range of literary texts of increasing length, e.g. stories, poems and scripts using literary devices studied so far for effect

7W7 Evaluate own and others' writing, suggesting improvements including making the writing more powerful and evaluating literary devices

Language

- As students this age have access to the internet and potentially to fake news, encourage volunteers to share some examples if appropriate.
- Ask how they found the pieces of news and what helped them realise they were fake. Encourage the class to mention or research ways to spot fake news.

Reading: A newspaper report page 27

Learning objectives

7R1 Ask and answer a range of questions about longer texts and summarise the main and supporting points

7R8 Read age-appropriate texts fluently and with understanding

Let's read

- Ask students to identify which parts of the report show that the writer took notes or made a recording of the interview. Check as a class.
- If time allows, have students use the text to make up the reporter's questions.
- Have volunteers say how biased they think this report is and why. Remind them to refer to the text to support their answers.

Reading: A newspaper report (continued) page 28

Learning objectives

7SL2 Express ideas, opinions and feelings with increasing detail and clarity, justifying own viewpoint and linking it to others' viewpoints

7R3 Understand the purpose of different parts of a text in a wide range of texts, including genres of fiction

7R4 Explore characters' feelings, personalities and motivations in increasing detail, referring to the text and relating to own experience or other reading

Let's talk

- Ask pairs or small groups to discuss the questions. Check as a class, helping students to think about the text as a whole and its purpose.
- You could ask additional questions for students to practise referring to the text to support their answers.

Reading and writing: Features of a newspaper report page 29

Learning objectives

7R1 Ask and answer a range of questions about longer texts and summarise the main and supporting points

7R6 Explore a range of literary features and discuss writers' intentions, beginning to give support from the text

7W11 Use a wide range of punctuation appropriately

7L1 Use a wide range of language forms appropriately

Let's read

- Before going through the Student Book text, refer students to the newspaper report on pages 27 and 28. Ask them to help you find features of this text type and take notes on the board. Remind them to justify their answers by referring to the newspaper report.
- Ask students to work in pairs and check if the features on the board match the text on page 29.
- Check as a class and go through the captions, confirming if they had been mentioned or noticed at the beginning of the lesson. Lead a discussion about how the features can aid people in following the text and how it is achieved.

Writing: Structuring paragraphs
page 30

Learning objectives

7W9 Write longer texts, grouping ideas in paragraphs and with an opening and a conclusion

7L6 Use a range of structural features for effect, e.g. dramatic effect, suspense

Activity

- If time allows, have pairs go back to the newspaper report on pages 27 and 28. Have them assign the main idea to each paragraph. They can choose to focus on one page each to work faster. Then they can choose one paragraph to find the main and supporting points.

Language: Active and passive voices
page 31

Learning objectives

7L1 Use a wide range of language forms appropriately

7L6 Use a range of structural features for effect, e.g. dramatic effect, suspense

7L7 Use Standard English accurately and at increasing length for a range of topics, purposes and audiences

Activity

- As students have learned about the differences between active and passive voice in previous levels, you can ask them to work in pairs and mindmap what they remember. This can help you gauge students' prior knowledge to determine if a revision lesson is needed or if you can challenge them with extra tasks.

Language: Open and closed questions
page 32

Learning objectives

7R4 Explore characters' feelings, personalities and motivations in increasing detail, referring to the text and relating to own experience or other reading

7L1 Use a wide range of language forms appropriately

7L7 Use Standard English accurately and at increasing length for a range of topics, purposes and audiences

Language

- As students have studied the differences between open and closed questions, invite volunteers to briefly explain the difference.
- As you go through the examples of closed questions, encourage students to make a follow-up question to get more information. Explain that sometimes a simple *Why, or why not?* is enough and demonstrate this. For example, ask a volunteer: *Do you like chocolate? Why or why not?*

Activity

- You may want to use the interview for students to write their newspaper report next lesson. If so, ask students to record or take notes of the interview.
- Students could also use this as the first part of the interview and keep their roles to ask more questions to complement the information for their report.

Writing: Writing a newspaper report from an interview
page 33

Learning objectives

7SL10 Listen and respond appropriately in a wide range of speaking activities

7SL11 Ask and answer a wide range of questions asking for detailed information and seeking clarification

7W5 Write a range of non-fiction text types for different audiences and purposes using appropriate features and adapting language for different audiences

7W7 Evaluate own and others' writing, suggesting improvements including making the writing more powerful and evaluating literary devices

7W9 Write longer texts, grouping ideas in paragraphs and with an opening and a conclusion

7L1 Use a wide range of language forms appropriately

Activity

- Optionally, you may wish to arrange a class visitor, such as a local sportsperson, who could be interviewed by the class or in groups.
- This writing task may need several sessions. For example, one session for writing questions, another for planning the write-up, another for writing up the interview.
- Students can use the Newspaper report write-up planner on Workbook page 22 to help them organise their ideas (this is also on page 60 of this Teacher's Guide).
- You can reinforce the work on self-correction by allowing students to correct their first draft. Remind them to check vocabulary, grammar, spelling and punctuation when they finish their newspaper report. Then ask them to go through it again and underline any aspects that can be improved; they can use the prompts in point 6 as a guide.

- Allow them to write a second draft to share with the rest of the class.
- Display the reports around the classroom and ask students to read two of them. Encourage them to say what they like about the reports they read. They can also mention some general aspects that could work better, but without naming authors. The idea is to get general feedback as a class.

Projects   pages 34–35

Project 1: Performance

Learning objectives

7SL9 Plan and deliver a presentation, adapting the content and language to the audience

7SL10 Listen and respond appropriately in a wide range of speaking activities

7SL12 Take turns when speaking in a range of longer, more complex exchanges, keeping the conversation going, and concluding it effectively

Project guidance

- If time allows, both projects can be completed in one session or in several sessions throughout the unit. You may prefer to choose one project for students to complete. Alternatively, you may wish to give students the choice of which project they would like to complete.
- If some students are working more than other group members, you can reassign the roles or tasks.
- Allow groups to work together to give feedback. Remind them to be respectful of everyone's work.
- Less confident students may benefit from having a checklist of features to improve their performance. You can create very simple guidelines with four or five points to bear in mind.
- Before students start working on the project, ask them to refer to their Project reflection notes of Unit 1. Tell them to think about what they can do better this time. Encourage them to add feedback to these notes about this unit performance after Reflection. They can also record what went well so that they can use this information in future projects.
- It would save time on this project if you provide a 1–2-minute range of video extracts for the students to use. Note that these clips should have their original audio deleted or at least muted.

Project 2: Writing

Learning objectives

7SL9 Plan and deliver a presentation, adapting the content and language to the audience

7SL13 Take part in group discussions and problem-solving activities and extended projects, working together to achieve an outcome

7W5 Write a range of non-fiction text types for different audiences and purposes using appropriate features and adapting language for different audiences

7W7 Evaluate own and others' writing, suggesting improvements including making the writing more powerful and evaluating literary devices

Project guidance

- For Project 2, have groups research the features of a fact file. Then have them vote for a poster, a booklet or an on-screen presentation; remind them to choose a format that is easy to manage as a group.
- Help students assess how much more input is required about the format or features and how much scaffolding is required; for example, the use of a template. They should also consider which images to include.
- You may want to keep developing self-correction by suggesting groups to write a first draft of their text, with no images yet. Ask them to check vocabulary, grammar, spelling and punctuation when they finish their fact file.
- Then ask them to go through the Unusual sports checklist and underline any aspects that can be improved. Allow them to make a corrected version for their presentation.

3 Mother Nature

Unit opener
page 36

Learning objectives

7SL1 Speak with confidence, fluency and accurate pronunciation on a wide range of familiar and unfamiliar topics

7SL2 Express ideas, opinions and feelings with increasing detail and clarity, justifying own viewpoint and linking it to others' viewpoints

7SL3 Describe a range of people, places and objects and events in detail using a range of mainly accurate language, choosing interesting language

7SL4 Speak freely, fluently and confidently and at increasing length in Creole and Standard English

7SL5 Use Creole and different registers of Standard English appropriately in a wide range of different contexts to express a wide range of feelings and ideas

7SL12 Take turns when speaking in a range of longer, more complex exchanges, keeping the conversation going, and concluding it effectively

Images and Let's talk

- Use the pictures and the Let's talk questions as a way to gauge students' prior knowledge on the topic, to determine how much detail you can go into, or whether further information is needed to introduce the topic.
- Ask students what they think when they hear the term *Mother Nature*. Prompt them so that they can expand their ideas. Have them look at the pictures and ask if any are similar to what they think about. Please note that discussing experiences of extreme weather such as hurricanes should be done sensitively. Only ask for willing participants to contribute.
- It may be a good idea to help students notice that negative experiences with nature can also bring positive aspects. For example, hurricane wind blows spores and seeds further inland from where they would normally fall; the seeds can replenish lost growth after fires and urbanisation.

Reading: Hurricane
page 37

Learning objectives

7SL7 Read aloud fluently and confidently, with appropriate expression, in a wide range of longer texts

7R1 Ask and answer a range of questions about longer texts and summarise the main and supporting points

7R5 Explore the language in a wide range of longer Creole and Standard English texts, e.g. poems, stories, age-appropriate novels and non-fiction texts

7R7 Talk about stories and poems they like in detail and give reasons, referring to the text

Let's read

- Assign a while-reading activity to help students focus on the poem as you read it aloud. For example, ask them to identify the rhyming words. This can help them activate prior knowledge about free verse; students learned about free verse in Level 5 Unit 6. (A free verse poem does not need a structure like other poems. It does not have a regular rhyme or rhythm. It sounds more like natural speech.)
- You can round up the activity by asking students which poetic devices they identify in 'Hurricane'.

Reading: Stormman
page 38

Learning objectives

7SL7 Read aloud fluently and confidently, with appropriate expression, in a wide range of longer texts

7R1 Ask and answer a range of questions about longer texts and summarise the main and supporting points

7R7 Talk about stories and poems they like in detail and give reasons, referring to the text

Let's read

- Have volunteers answer some quick questions about the poem before reading it. For example: *Who wrote the poem?* (Grace Nicholls) *How many stanzas does it have?* (11) *What type of poem is it?* (Free verse)

Stretch

- Try to draw out ideas about authorial intent, for example: *Maybe because hurricanes are chaotic and messy, the poems don't have patterns or rhymes.* Encourage students to give their views, emphasising that there are no right or wrong answers.

Language: Using figurative language page 39

Learning objective

7R6 Explore a range of literary features and discuss writers' intentions, beginning to give support from the text

Let's talk

- If possible, have some Student Books Level 6 available. Allow students to check Unit 6 if they need help remembering the poetic devices. Another option is to check dictionaries.

Activity

- For question 3, students could read their examples without saying what they are personifying. Allow the rest of the class to guess and justify their answers.

Speaking and listening: A group discussion to compare poems page 40

Learning objectives

7SL1 Speak with confidence, fluency and accurate pronunciation on a wide range of familiar and unfamiliar topics

7SL2 Express ideas, opinions and feelings with increasing detail and clarity, justifying own viewpoint and linking it to others' viewpoints

7SL10 Listen and respond appropriately in a wide range of speaking activities

7SL12 Take turns when speaking in a range of longer, more complex exchanges, keeping the conversation going, and concluding it effectively

7SL13 Take part in group discussions and problem-solving activities and extended projects, working together to achieve an outcome

Activity

- The aim of the 'discussion points' cards is to encourage students to discuss the two poems. The discussion points should provoke debate rather than focus on comprehension. Here are some suggested discussion points:
  - The poem 'Hurricane' is better at expressing the power of Mother Nature than 'Stormman'. Discuss.
  - The poem 'Stormman' expresses better how the poet feels about the power of Mother Nature. Discuss.
  - The structure, rhythm and rhyme of each poem suits what they are about. Discuss.
  - The figurative language used in 'Hurricane' is more interesting and attention-grabbing than in 'Stormman'. Discuss.
  - Overall, 'Stormman' is better than 'Hurricane'. Discuss.
- If you do not have enough 'discussion points' sets, you can display or write each point on the board for all groups to discuss at the same time.
- Elicit what a chairperson does in a group. Ask students who have not been chairperson before to take the role this time.

Let's talk

- If time allows, have groups discuss one or two points again but this time applying the improvements discussed.

Language: Word choice page 41

Learning objectives

7L2 Use a wide range of interesting and powerful new words

7L3 Recognise and use a wide range of synonyms and antonyms

Activity

- Prepare the card sets beforehand.
- For 'Find your synonym', make sets of four cards of synonyms with a mix of different word types, for example, adjectives, verbs and so on.
- For 'Find your antonym', make paired sets of antonyms (e.g. light/dark).
- Allow the students to group themselves with little interference. Monitor and ask questions about their thoughts and decisions.
- Have thesauruses available for question 3.

Language: Punctuation: Hyphens page 42

Learning objective

7W11 Use a wide range of punctuation appropriately

Activity

- Check students understand the set rules when using hyphens. However, it is worth emphasising that students should not be afraid to use a hyphen if it makes a word clearer and easier to read and understand. For example, *co-operate* and *cooperate* are both easy to read and understand, but it may be better to write *de-ice* rather than *deice*.

Vocabulary: Building vocabulary
page 43

Learning objectives

7W6 Write a range of literary texts of increasing length, e.g. stories, poems and scripts using literary devices studied so far for effect

7W10 Use appropriate layout when writing a wide range of longer texts, e.g. stories, poems, information texts, presentations, scripts

7L2 Use a wide range of interesting and powerful new words

7L3 Recognise and use a wide range of synonyms and antonyms

Activity

- For the 'Hotseat taboo', prepare a suitable list of words in advance. This can also be played as a game with two teams. Remind students not to use gestures.
- Explain that the diamante poem should show the word classes required for each line. For example, *first line = one noun*, *second line = two adjectives*, and so on. You can write the sample poem on the board and use colours or arrows to make this clearer.
- You can change any of the games for 'Wall words' if suitable. Prepare many cards with words that are not visible from a distance so that students find and read them. The words should be a mix of word types and should be tailored to the level of the class to challenge them. Try to include some hyphenated compound words. They could be words related to the theme of Mother Nature or a different subject.
- Display the cards around the classroom.
- Have students move around and write a sentence using one of the words. Repeat this for a few more words.
- Alternatively, students choose three more wall words to write a sentence that uses all three of them.

Reading: Bush fire
page 44

Learning objectives

7SL7 Read aloud fluently and confidently, with appropriate expression, in a wide range of longer texts

7R1 Ask and answer a range of questions about longer texts and summarise the main and supporting points

7R6 Explore a range of literary features and discuss writers' intentions, beginning to give support from the text

Let's read

- Read the poem aloud and have students follow along in a quiet voice. Have them identify which sounds repeat the most.
- Ask: *Are these sounds soft or strong? What do they remind you of? Why do you think the author chose these words or sounds?* Explain that there are no wrong answers.

Let's talk

- Check answers as a class. If necessary, explain these are types of dance. If time allows, show some videos and ask students why they think the author chose these dances to describe the fire.

Reading: Frost and Fog
page 45

Learning objectives

7SL2 Express ideas, opinions and feelings with increasing detail and clarity, justifying own viewpoint and linking it to others' viewpoints

7R1 Ask and answer a range of questions about longer texts and summarise the main and supporting points

Let's talk

- Check answers and encourage students to discuss the poems further. For example, ask: *Do you understand the poems? What do you think of them? What do you like or dislike about them? Which one do you prefer and why? What's the difference between frost and snow?*

Language

- As these poetic devices have been taught previously, you can write the terms on the board and have students describe or exemplify them. They can use the Student Book poems to find some examples.
- You may also want to check or teach how to pronounce *enjambment*: /ɪnˈdʒæmbmənt/.

Language: More figurative language
page 46

Learning objectives

7R6 Explore a range of literary features and discuss writers' intentions, beginning to give support from the text

7L1 Use a wide range of language forms appropriately

Language

- Write *figurative language* on the board and elicit some examples. Students may go back to Student Book page 39 if they need help.

- Write *simile* and *metaphor* on the board and elicit how they are different. You can remind students a simile says something is *like* something else and a metaphor says something *is* something else.
- You can ask students if they use some similes or metaphors in everyday life; encourage them to share some examples. Help them analyse why they use these and their effect.
- Ask how different the effect and meaning of some phrases is from the literal meaning.

Language: Loanwords   page 47

Learning objectives
7W1 Spell most words correctly and proofread own and others' work for accuracy

7L2 Use a wide range of interesting and powerful new words

7L5 Use knowledge of word formation to understand and use new words

Language and Let's read
- Quickly check that students understand the word *loan*.
- List *cheetah, flamenco* and *haunch* on the board and ask what they have in common. If students cannot guess correctly, explain the concept of loanwords.
- List the languages *French, Hindi and Spanish* to the right of the first word list, for the class to match each word with its origin language. If suitable, tell students that *denim* comes from the French words *de Nîmes*, meaning *from Nîmes* (Nîmes, pronounced *neem*, is a French city).
- Ask: *How many more languages can you name apart from the ones mentioned in the text?*
- Some possible answers: Arabic, Chinese, Dutch, German, Papiamento, Portuguese, Tamil, Urdu.

Activity
- You can have pairs discuss the original language of the underlined words in the text.
- Check as a class: kindergarten – German; ballet – French; guitar – Spanish; biology – Greek; pizzas – Italian; coleslaw – Dutch; ketchup – Malay; trek – Dutch; savannah – Taino; giraffe – Arabic; husband – Norwegian; chess – Persian; cruise – Dutch; pyjamas – Urdu; bungalow – Hindi.
- Question 2 can be done in small groups. Students list the original language of each word. They earn 1 point for every correct answer; the student with the most points wins the game.
- Read aloud the answers for students to check: reggae – Jamaican Creole; sauna – Swedish; tsunami – Japanese; history – Greek; piano – Italian; yoga – Sanskrit; jubilee – Hebrew; coffee – Turkish; alligator – Spanish; shampoo – Hindi.
- You can organise a spelling bee competition with the loanwords through the rest of the unit. It can be done at the end of every lesson.

Speaking and listening: A jigsaw discussion about Mother Nature   page 48

Learning objectives
7SL1 Speak with confidence, fluency and accurate pronunciation on a wide range of familiar and unfamiliar topics

7SL3 Describe a range of people, places and objects and events in detail using a range of mainly accurate language, choosing interesting language

7SL11 Ask and answer a wide range of questions asking for detailed information and seeking clarification

7SL12 Take turns when speaking in a range of longer, more complex exchanges, keeping the conversation going, and concluding it effectively

7SL13 Take part in group discussions and problem-solving activities and extended projects, working together to achieve an outcome

Activity
- Elicit what students would like to learn in this activity and use the information to select aspects to research. If suitable, you can vote as a class to choose the top five aspects to assign.

Writing: Writing a poem about Mother Nature   page 49

Learning objectives
7W3 Plan and develop creative writing in a range of different genres of fiction, non-fiction and types of poem, using the most appropriate planning method

7W6 Write a range of literary texts of increasing length, e.g. stories, poems and scripts using literary devices studied so far for effect

7W7 Evaluate own and others' writing, suggesting improvements including making the writing more powerful and evaluating literary devices

7L2 Use a wide range of interesting and powerful new words

Activity
- Students can use the 'Mother Nature' poem planner on Workbook page 32 to help them organise their ideas (this is also on page 61 of this Teacher's Guide).

Feedback
- Have students answer the questions and then use this information to write a paragraph giving feedback. Remind them to start and finish it with a positive comment.

Project 1: Performance

Learning objectives

7SL9 Plan and deliver a presentation, adapting the content and language to the audience

7SL13 Take part in group discussions and problem-solving activities and extended projects, working together to achieve an outcome

7W7 Evaluate own and others' writing, suggesting improvements including making the writing more powerful and evaluating literary devices

Project guidance

- If time allows, both projects can be completed in one session or in several sessions throughout the unit. You may prefer to choose one project for students to complete. Alternatively, you may wish to give students the choice of which project they would like to complete.
- If some students are working more than other group members, you can reassign the roles or tasks.
- Allow groups to work together to give feedback. Remind them to be respectful of everyone's work.
- Less confident students may benefit from having a checklist of features to improve their performance. You can create very simple guidelines with four or five points to bear in mind.
- Before students start working on the project, ask them to refer to their Project reflection notes. Tell them to think about what they can do better this time. Encourage them to add feedback to these notes about this performance after Reflection.

Project 2: Writing

Learning objectives

7SL13 Take part in group discussions and problem-solving activities and extended projects, working together to achieve an outcome

7W6 Write a range of literary texts of increasing length, e.g. stories, poems and scripts using literary devices studied so far for effect

7W7 Evaluate own and others' writing, suggesting improvements including making the writing more powerful and evaluating literary devices

Project guidance

- You may want to display on the board a Call and response folk song from Level 6 Unit 9 to explain how a tapestry poem works.
- Explain that for this project, each pair of lines could be one at a time, in groups or in any order they decide to do it; the only criterion is that all 16 lines from the two poems must be used.

Suspense

Unit opener
page 54

Learning objectives

7SL1 Speak with confidence, fluency and accurate pronunciation on a wide range of familiar and unfamiliar topics

7SL2 Express ideas, opinions and feelings with increasing detail and clarity, justifying own viewpoint and linking it to others' viewpoints

7SL3 Describe a range of people, places and objects and events in detail using a range of mainly accurate language, choosing interesting language

7SL4 Speak freely, fluently and confidently and at increasing length in Creole and Standard English

7SL5 Use Creole and different registers of Standard English appropriately in a wide range of different contexts to express a wide range of feelings and ideas

7SL12 Take turns when speaking in a range of longer, more complex exchanges, keeping the conversation going, and concluding it effectively

Images and Let's talk

- Use the pictures and the Let's talk questions as a way to gauge students' prior knowledge on the topic, to determine how much detail you can go into, or whether further information is needed to introduce the topic.
- Divide the class into small teams. Write the unit title on the board and give them one minute to write as many words in English using the letters of *suspense* as possible: *up, us, pen(s), see(s), sue(s), Sue, sun(s), use(s), ensue, sense, unsee,* and so on.
- Check the answers of the team with the most words for the others to check. Award one point for every correct word. The group with the most points wins the game.
- Check any other words that might have not been mentioned.
- Ask volunteers to say what they think about when they hear or read the word *suspense*.

Listening: A night in the jungle
page 55

Learning objectives

7SL2 Express ideas, opinions and feelings with increasing detail and clarity, justifying own viewpoint and linking it to others' viewpoints

7SL8 Plan, write and act a scene from life or fiction, acting convincingly

7R4 Explore characters' feelings, personalities and motivations in increasing detail, referring to the text and relating to own experience or other reading

7R7 Talk about stories and poems they like in detail and give reasons, referring to the text

Let's listen

- Tell students that you will read something aloud for them to summarise what they hear.
- Read aloud: *It is the holidays, and Omar and his brother Ahmed are staying with their grandparents, who run an ecolodge in the rainforest for tourists. Omar has not been to the lodge before. He and his brother are sharing a room. After a long journey and first day, Omar is ready for bed.*
- Invite a volunteer to summarise what they heard. If necessary, ask some comprehension questions.
- Explain that students will hear the first part of a suspense story. Encourage volunteers to predict what the story will be about. Let students listen to the first part of the story to check if any volunteer guessed correctly.

Activity

- The focus is to do some imaginative work from the audio stimulus as students achieve the learning objectives. The story is deliberately left on a cliffhanger here to encourage that.
- Try to draw out reactions to the role-plays, encouraging students to comment on whether the role-plays were successful at conveying and building tension and suspense.
- You may wish to limit the number of role-plays performed.

Reading: A night in the jungle (continued) — page 56

Learning objectives

7R2 Understand the purpose of a wide range of different texts, including different genres of fiction

7R3 Understand the purpose of different parts of a text in a wide range of texts, including genres of fiction

7R6 Explore a range of literary features and discuss writers' intentions, beginning to give support from the text

7R8 Read age-appropriate texts fluently and with understanding

Let's read

- Elicit what the first part of the story was about to tune in students to the activity.
- Assign a short while-reading task to help students focus. You can ask which characters are mentioned or parts of the text students consider suspenseful.

Activity

- Use question d to help students to see the link between how the paragraph organisation is designed to build tension and suspense to a climax and then release the tension in the final paragraph of this part.

Reading: A night in the jungle (continued) — page 57

Learning objectives

7R3 Understand the purpose of different parts of a text in a wide range of texts, including genres of fiction

7R6 Explore a range of literary features and discuss writers' intentions, beginning to give support from the text

7R8 Read age-appropriate texts fluently and with understanding

Let's read and Let's talk

- Elicit a summary of the story so far.
- Adapt the Let's talk questions from page 56: *How does the writer build or release the tension and suspense in the second part of the story? What role does each paragraph play in achieving this?*
- Ask students to read the final part of the story on their own trying to answer the same questions.

Writing: Descriptive writing — page 58

Learning objectives

7W7 Evaluate own and others' writing, suggesting improvements including making the writing more powerful and evaluating literary devices

7L2 Use a wide range of interesting and powerful new words

Language

- Elicit stories students like or that they have read recently.
- Have them sit in small groups as you write this question on the board: *How can a writer make the reader feel as if they are there in a scene?*
- Ask students to discuss and allow them to refer to their Student Book stories if necessary.
- Check answers as a class and direct students to the Descriptive writing text to find any of the mentioned features.

Language: Adverbials — page 59

Learning objectives

7W4 Create stories using a range of techniques, e.g. different points of view, creating suspense

7L1 Use a wide range of language forms appropriately

Activity

- For question 2, alternatively, you can write one adverbial on a card each. Divide the class into small groups and assign some cards at random for them to say or write sentences starting with each adverbial.
- You can redistribute the cards and repeat the activity as many times as you consider suitable.
- You can ask the volunteers to write the sentences on the board and check as a class to foster simple peer-correction.

Stretch

- Answer: *as time stood still*, because it is the only option that contains a verb (*stood*). As a fronted adverbial, it would therefore also be a subordinate clause.

Reading: In the dark — page 60

Learning objectives

7R4 Explore characters' feelings, personalities and motivations in increasing detail, referring to the text and relating to own experience or other reading

7R8 Read age-appropriate texts fluently and with understanding

Let's read

- Divide the class into groups of five and assign a role to each to act out the story: the narrator, Anthony, Kemar, Jade and Raeni.
- Let them read the text on their own first so that they can identify which parts they will read. You may want the same groups to answer the Let's talk questions.

Reading: In the dark (continued)
page 61

Learning objective
7R6 Explore a range of literary features and discuss writers' intentions, beginning to give support from the text

Let's read

- Read the first line aloud and ask who *he* is. Direct students back to page 60 to check their answer.
- Have students work in the same groups as in the previous lesson. They can keep or change their roles if they all agree.

Language

- You may want to expand on this topic by explaining that in fiction there are no accidents or extra information. Everything, even the smallest detail, is there for a reason (unlike in real life).

Reading and speaking: In the dark (continued)
page 62

Learning objective
7R1 Ask and answer a range of questions about longer texts and summarise the main and supporting points

Let's read

- Ask volunteers to help you recap the story before reading this next part of the story.
- If time allows, ask: *What do you think the writer's intention is?*
- Suggested answer: to build tension and create suspense.
- Ask: *How does the writer do this?*
- Suggested answer: by making the environment more restrictive and then suddenly dark due to an unforeseen event.

Reading and speaking: In the dark (continued)
page 63

Learning objective
7R7 Talk about stories and poems they like in detail and give reasons, referring to the text

Let's read

- Invite volunteers to summarise what has happened in the story so far.
- List some comprehension questions on the board. For example: *What fell on Jade? Why did Anthony and Jade clamber to their feet? Why are Raeni's parents in an ambulance? Why does Kemar stink? Why did the police officer say the warning signs are there for a reason?*
- Ask pairs or small groups to make up the next part of the story. The only restriction is that it answers all the questions on the board. The story can be oral or written.
- Then have students compare how similar to or different from the actual text their story is.

Writing: Building tension and creating suspense
pages 64–65

Learning objective
7R6 Explore a range of literary features and discuss writers' intentions, beginning to give support from the text

Language

- As you go through each technique with the class, ask how effective they think each one is. Encourage volunteers to find examples in previously read stories to support their answers.
- Students can make posters for each technique. Assign one to each group. Ask them to include a short explanation and three examples from different stories. Display their work around the classroom.
- If time allows, ask students to work in pairs or small groups. Ask them to use the power-of-three technique to describe:
  - a piece of homework recently completed
  - a list of shopping items
  - someone carrying out a task.
- If necessary, model one example: *My maths homework was interesting, challenging and fun.*

Language: Using ellipses and single dashes for suspense · page 66

Learning objective
7W11 Use a wide range of punctuation appropriately

Let's talk
- Lead this activity and help address any misconceptions and provide further guidance in relation to question 3.

Writing: Writing suspense stories · page 67

Learning objectives
7W1 Spell most words correctly and proofread own and others' work for accuracy

7W3 Plan and develop creative writing in a range of different genres of fiction, non-fiction and types of poem, using the most appropriate planning method

7W4 Create stories using a range of techniques, e.g. different points of view, creating suspense

7W7 Evaluate own and others' writing, suggesting improvements including making the writing more powerful and evaluating literary devices

7W9 Write longer texts, grouping ideas in paragraphs and with an opening and a conclusion

7L6 Use a range of structural features for effect, e.g. dramatic effect, suspense

Activity
- Students can use the Suspense story planner on Workbook page 42 to help them organise their ideas (this is also on page 62 of this Teacher's Guide).
- You may want to reinforce the idea of self-correction by allowing students to correct their own first draft. Remind them to check vocabulary, grammar, spelling and punctuation when they finish their story.
- Then ask them to go through the Suspense story techniques checklist and underline any aspects that can be improved. Remind them that they can't check or make corrections before they write; writers should correct the mistakes that have been identified.
- Allow students to write a second draft for a partner to check. The corrections would then become their final version that would be displayed or used for the class book.
- Remind students that it is a good idea to start and finish the feedback with positive comments.

Projects · pages 68–69

Project 1: Writing

Learning objectives
7SL8 Plan, write and act a scene from life or fiction, acting convincingly

7SL13 Take part in group discussions and problem-solving activities and extended projects, working together to achieve an outcome

7W6 Write a range of literary texts of increasing length, e.g. stories, poems and scripts using literary devices studied so far for effect

7W7 Evaluate own and others' writing, suggesting improvements including making the writing more powerful and evaluating literary devices

7W10 Use appropriate layout when writing a wide range of longer texts, e.g. stories, poems, information texts, presentations, scripts

Project guidance
- If time allows, both projects can be completed in one session or in several sessions throughout the unit. You may prefer to choose one project for students to complete. Alternatively, you may wish to give students the choice of which project they would like to complete.
- If some students are working more than other group members, you can reassign the roles or tasks.
- Allow groups to work together to give feedback. Remind them to be respectful of everyone's work.
- Less confident students may benefit from having a checklist of features to improve their performance. You can create very simple guidelines with four or five points to bear in mind.
- Before students start working on the project, ask them to refer to their Project reflection notes. Tell them to think about what they can do better this time. Encourage them to add feedback to these notes about this performance after Reflection.
- Less confident students can work in pairs or small groups.
- Students may go back to Unit 1 and check the playscripts to use as a model; the Features of a playscript on page 13 can be useful as well.
- You may want to keep developing self- and peer-correction by using two drafts and a final version of the playscript.

Project 2: Performance

Learning objectives

7SL8 Plan, write and act a scene from life or fiction, acting convincingly

7SL12 Take turns when speaking in a range of longer, more complex exchanges, keeping the conversation going, and concluding it effectively

7SL13 Take part in group discussions and problem-solving activities and extended projects, working together to achieve an outcome

- Support students in finding ways to learn their lines. Explain that repetition is essential.
- Encourage students to mindmap ideas to help them remember their lines.
- Students can highlight their lines in the playscript copies to visualise them easily.
- They can also write their lines on index cards so that they are easy to carry; students can read them whenever they have time available, which will help them memorise the text.
- Consider splitting performances up over a number of sessions to allow students to appreciate each other's performances without too much repetition.

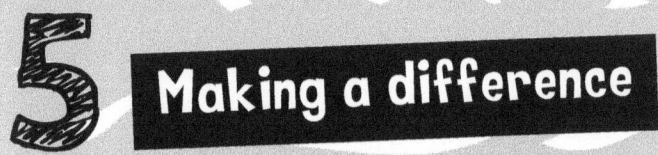

5 Making a difference

Learning objectives

7SL1 Speak with confidence, fluency and accurate pronunciation on a wide range of familiar and unfamiliar topics

7SL2 Express ideas, opinions and feelings with increasing detail and clarity, justifying own viewpoint and linking it to others' viewpoints

7SL3 Describe a range of people, places and objects and events in detail using a range of mainly accurate language, choosing interesting language

7SL4 Speak freely, fluently and confidently and at increasing length in Creole and Standard English

7SL5 Use Creole and different registers of Standard English appropriately in a wide range of different contexts to express a wide range of feelings and ideas

7SL12 Take turns when speaking in a range of longer, more complex exchanges, keeping the conversation going, and concluding it effectively

Images and Let's talk

- Use the pictures and the Let's talk questions as a way to gauge students' prior knowledge on the topic, to determine how much detail you can go into, or whether further information is needed to introduce the topic.
- Ask students how they think the unit title and the photos are connected.
- Explain where the images are from and what they show. Clockwise, from top left:
  - red-mud ponds, a by-product of bauxite mining in Jamaica
  - deforestation in the Caribbean
  - the devastating effect that warmer seas and increased hurricane and storm damage are having on coral reefs around the world
  - students cleaning a polluted beach in Jamaica
  - sign for Jamaica Environment Trust Recycling Collection Depot
  - children in Bridgetown, Barbados, participating in a climate walk and rally on World Children's Day.

Learning objectives

7SL7 Read aloud fluently and confidently, with appropriate expression, in a wide range of longer texts

7R8 Read age-appropriate texts fluently and with understanding

Let's read

- Write the heading *Climate change* and draw a KWL three-column chart on poster paper so that you can keep it for next lesson. (This activity can be used with any text that can activate prior knowledge.)
- Note down what students know (K) and what they would like to know (W) about climate change. Have students read the Q&A and check if what they know is true or mentioned. Do not check answers as a class yet.
- Have volunteers record what they learned in the corresponding column (L). Explain that this is just the first part of the text and that they might get more information next lesson. In the meantime, students can look for the information they would like to know.

Learning objectives

7SL7 Read aloud fluently and confidently, with appropriate expression, in a wide range of longer texts

7R1 Ask and answer a range of questions about longer texts and summarise the main and supporting points

Let's read

- Display the *Climate change* KWL chart from the previous lesson and go through the content. Ask volunteers to share any new information they have looked up and add it.
- Have students read the second part of the Q&A and invite volunteers to record what they learned in the corresponding column (L).
- Highlight the information in the W column that was not mentioned in the text. Divide the class into small groups and assign them one topic to research for the next lesson.

- Read the last sentence of the text aloud and have a class discussion about ways they can make an impact. Remind students that all actions, big or small, help. Help them focus on things that are achievable and age-appropriate.

Let's talk

- For question 4, help students to realise that Sydney's aim is to inform and persuade, which links in with later activities and the main text type in this unit.

Speaking and listening: Jigsaw discussion about environmental issues   page 73

Learning objectives

7SL1 Speak with confidence, fluency and accurate pronunciation on a wide range of familiar and unfamiliar topics

7SL3 Describe a range of people, places and objects and events in detail using a range of mainly accurate language, choosing interesting language

7SL11 Ask and answer a wide range of questions asking for detailed information and seeking clarification

7SL12 Take turns when speaking in a range of longer, more complex exchanges, keeping the conversation going, and concluding it effectively

7SL13 Take part in group discussions and problem-solving activities and extended projects, working together to achieve an outcome

Activity

- Remind students they have done this 'jigsaw discussion' activity in Unit 3, Mother Nature (page 48). Elicit instructions to check understanding.
- If time allows, have groups work on two drafts and a final version to foster self- and peer-correction.
- It can be highly motivating for students to share their work with people outside their class. If possible, ask colleagues that teach the same level if you can all share the environmental issues work. You can exchange topic webs, tables or leaflets for the classes to read. Alternatively, you could share the work on the school bulletin board.

Language: Making adjectives from nouns   page 74

Learning objectives

7W2 Develop strategies including using known spelling patterns to predict spelling of new words

7L4 Use a wide range of prefixes and suffixes with verbs, nouns, adjectives and adverbs

Language

- Before going through the Student Book information, elicit what a suffix is. If time allows, allow pairs to work on a brief explanation. Students have studied suffixes throughout previous levels so this is a good opportunity to check understanding. For example, a suffix is a group of letters that we add to the end of a word to change its meaning (and function in a sentence).

Activity

- To get students ready for the next lesson, you can play a game to activate prior knowledge about prefixes and suffixes.
- Divide the class into small groups. Write the nouns of question 2a on the board. Have groups write as many words as they can adding prefixes and suffixes to the roots. Ask two groups to exchange their list of words to check. Each correct word earns one point. The group with the most points wins the game.

Language: Less common prefixes   page 75

Learning objectives

7L4 Use a wide range of prefixes and suffixes with verbs, nouns, adjectives and adverbs

7L5 Use knowledge of word formation to understand and use new words

Language

- Before going through the Student Book information, elicit what a prefix is: a group of letters that we add to the beginning of a word to change its meaning (and function in a sentence). Then, if time allows, copy the Prefix column onto the board. Challenge small groups to work out their meaning and add one or two examples. Tell them to check against the Student Book table.

Activity

- As students may not use many of the words in the box regularly, encourage them to make up sentences to practise them. You can allocate five minutes to prefix and suffix work where students share their sentences. If possible, use a large sheet of paper to record them and keep them on display.

Reading: Persuasive writing page 76

Learning objectives
7R2 Understand the purpose of a wide range of different texts, including different genres of fiction

7R8 Read age-appropriate texts fluently and with understanding

Let's read
- Ask students to list any vocabulary questions they may have as they read the letter. Then ask them to work in small groups to try to answer the questions. Have some dictionaries available for students to check as necessary.

Language and reading
Features of a persuasive text page 77

Learning objective
7R5 Explore the language in a wide range of longer Creole and Standard English texts, e.g. poems, stories, age-appropriate novels and non-fiction texts

Language and Let's talk
- Alternatively, you can go through the Let's talk questions before the Language input. Then as you go through this section, you can merge it with the Activity.
- Read aloud one of the features and give small groups only a minute to find examples in Maya's letter. Doing the activity against time gives students a sense of competition that helps them focus better.

Activity
- Explain to students that this is an activity to activate prior knowledge as these are features that they have come across before. You may need to help students identify some features.

Language and writing: Purpose,
form, audience and tone page 78

Learning objective
7R2 Understand the purpose of a wide range of different texts, including different genres of fiction

Language
- As you go through the text or check students' work, you can complement the information. Explain that persuading someone is different from instructing someone (purpose); writing an advert for a film is different from writing a review of a film (form); writing an email to a grandparent is different from writing an email to a boss (audience); and that using informal, personal language to write a diary entry is different from using formal Standard English to write a job application (tone).

- More confident students can work on their own but as this is a long text and students need to process the information, you can also use jigsaw reading. Divide the class into groups of four and assign one aspect to each. They should read their part and then explain to the rest of the groups what they learned. Allow them to check their text if they are unsure about their explanation.
- Explain that PFAT stands for Purpose, Form, Audience and Tone, and is helpful to identify everything about any reading text and also prior to writing.

Reading: Facts and opinions page 79

Learning objectives
7R3 Understand the purpose of different parts of a text in a wide range of texts, including genres of fiction

7R8 Read age-appropriate texts fluently and with understanding

Let's read and Let's talk
- To save time, you can use the Let's talk questions as a while-reading activity. Then students can check their answers in pairs.
- Ask pairs to think of a title for the paragraph. Tell them they have to support their choice. Remind them that titles should reflect the content of the text but they also need to be attention-grabbing and easy to read.
- Ask three pairs to work together and choose their best title. Tell them to write it on the board. Have individual students raise their hand for their favourite title.

Language: Linking
ideas using connectives page 80

Learning objective
7L1 Use a wide range of language forms appropriately

Language
- Before going through the Student Book information, elicit what the function of a connective is. Students have studied and used different kinds of connectives throughout previous levels so this is a good opportunity to ask about different purposes of connectives. Use the Student Book information to consolidate learning.

Activity
- You may want to take learning further and encourage students or pairs to rewrite the sentences from question 2 with other connectives they know. They can even change the meaning of the sentence.

Language: Personal and impersonal tones
page 81

Learning objective
7R5 Explore the language in a wide range of longer Creole and Standard English texts, e.g. poems, stories, age-appropriate novels and non-fiction texts

Language
- Start the lesson by saying a simple sentence in different tones, for example: *Close the door*. You can start saying it worriedly and then angrily. Then you could vary the words slightly to make the sentence more formal and then very informal.
- Encourage students to say what the differences between the sentences are. Explain that in written texts the reader cannot see the author so the author needs to use words to convey what they mean.

Let's talk and Tip
- Ask pairs to discuss why persuasive writing often uses a mix of personal and impersonal tones. Check as a class and help them reflect that the ultimate purpose of persuasive writing is to convince people so the writer uses different tones to achieve it.

Reading, speaking and listening: Taking action for the environment
page 82

Learning objective
7SL2 Express ideas, opinions and feelings with increasing detail and clarity, justifying own viewpoint and linking it to others' viewpoints

Let's talk
- Check answers as a class. Remind students that, if they want to help, it is a good idea to identify and persuade someone with power to take action.

Writing: Writing a persuasive letter
page 83

Learning objectives
7W3 Plan and develop creative writing in a range of different genres of fiction, non-fiction and types of poem, using the most appropriate planning method

7W5 Write a range of non-fiction text types for different audiences and purposes using appropriate features and adapting language for different audiences

7W7 Evaluate own and others' writing, suggesting improvements including making the writing more powerful and evaluating literary devices

7W8 Write legibly and with appropriate speed and fluency

Activity
- Students can use the Persuasive letter planner on Workbook page 52 to organise their ideas (this is also on page 63 of this Teacher's Guide).
- Suggest using the Persuasive letter checklist as a guide while writing their first draft. Remind them to make sure their handwriting is legible. Encourage them to check this draft for spelling, punctuation, vocabulary or grammar mistakes.
- Allow them to write a second draft for a partner to check. Encourage them to leave enough space between lines to allow partners to add notes.
- Remind students that they need to check their feedback and assess their partner's suggestions. Monitor and help as necessary. Have students write their final version on a separate piece of paper that can be displayed on the walls for everyone to read.

Projects
pages 84–85

Project 1: Writing

Learning objectives
7SL13 Take part in group discussions and problem-solving activities and extended projects, working together to achieve an outcome

7W3 Plan and develop creative writing in a range of different genres of fiction, non-fiction and types of poem, using the most appropriate planning method

7W5 Write a range of non-fiction text types for different audiences and purposes using appropriate features and adapting language for different audiences

7W7 Evaluate own and others' writing, suggesting improvements including making the writing more powerful and evaluating literary devices

7W10 Use appropriate layout when writing a wide range of longer texts, e.g. stories, poems, information texts, presentations, scripts

Project guidance
- If time allows, both projects can be completed in one session or in several sessions throughout the unit. You may prefer to ask some students to complete Project 1 only.
- If some students are working more than other group members, you can reassign the roles or tasks.
- You can group students based on their strengths to make sure they can all share out the writing and illustrating fairly.
- Encourage them to research what makes a fact file successful. They may remember work they have done in previous levels. Remind them to use the Fact file and campaign planning checklist when planning to make sure they have all the necessary features.

- You may want to keep developing self- and peer-correction by using two drafts and a final version of the fact file.

Project 2: Performance

Learning objectives

7SL9 Plan and deliver a presentation, adapting the content and language to the audience

7SL11 Ask and answer a wide range of questions asking for detailed information and seeking clarification

7SL13 Take part in group discussions and problem-solving activities and extended projects, working together to achieve an outcome

- To save time, you may not want to wait for the campaign materials of Project 1 to be on display for groups to write their survey. Remind students that surveys need to be short and efficient to gather the most information possible.
- Less confident students may benefit from having a checklist of features to improve their performance. You can create very simple guidelines with four or five points to bear in mind.
- Before students start working on the project, ask them to refer to their previous Project reflection notes. Tell them to think about what they can do better this time. Encourage them to add feedback to these notes about this performance after Reflection.

6 Creating characters

Learning objectives

7SL1 Speak with confidence, fluency and accurate pronunciation on a wide range of familiar and unfamiliar topics

7SL2 Express ideas, opinions and feelings with increasing detail and clarity, justifying own viewpoint and linking it to others' viewpoints

7SL3 Describe a range of people, places and objects and events in detail using a range of mainly accurate language, choosing interesting language

7SL4 Speak freely, fluently and confidently and at increasing length in Creole and Standard English

7SL5 Use Creole and different registers of Standard English appropriately in a wide range of different contexts to express a wide range of feelings and ideas

7SL12 Take turns when speaking in a range of longer, more complex exchanges, keeping the conversation going, and concluding it effectively

Images and Let's talk

- Use the pictures and the Let's talk questions as a way to gauge students' prior knowledge on the topic, to determine how much detail you can go into, or whether further information is needed to introduce the topic.
- Check the answers to Let's talk as a class. If time allows, tell students that you have the characters' brief that the authors used for writing this series. Tell them to compare how different the information is from what they know about the characters:
  ○ Aiden is sociable, smiling, curious and loves to climb trees; interested in nature and getting out into the countryside; attends the local Church of God.
  ○ Latoya is tall, wiry, athletic – interested in track and field; lives with grandparents, so helps with the yard/growing vegetables; an Anglican, Latoya loves attending church camps and telling stories.
  ○ Kwame loves singing, music and riding his bike; he is in the choir at school and church; has lots of brothers and sisters, so can be precocious to try and get attention.
  ○ Priya goes to a Hindu school – Baal Vikas is the big dance comp, so she loves music and trad dance; likes baking cakes and helps with preparing family meals. Her roti rocks; at weekends she goes to temple and helps in her community – taking meals to older people.
  ○ Omar likes playing with branded building blocks; goes with his older brother to help with charity work – helping less fortunate people; likes visiting the Masjid for prayers and learning from the Imam.
  ○ Maya is a talented gymnast – she practises hard most days; she is a Catholic and lives in a town near the capital city; her father is away for business so she spends most of her time at home when she is not training.

Learning objectives

7R1 Ask and answer a range of questions about longer texts and summarise the main and supporting points

7R4 Explore characters' feelings, personalities and motivations in increasing detail, referring to the text and relating to own experience or other reading

7R8 Read age-appropriate texts fluently and with understanding

Let's talk

- If time allows, have pairs list physical features of each character. Have them draw a character each and then compare their work with another pair's drawings.
- Display the pictures, grouping them by character. Discuss as a class how similar or different they are.

Learning objectives

7SL3 Describe a range of people, places and objects and events in detail using a range of mainly accurate language, choosing interesting language

7R1 Ask and answer a range of questions about longer texts and summarise the main and supporting points

7R4 Explore characters' feelings, personalities and motivations in increasing detail, referring to the text and relating to own experience or other reading

Language

- Ask students to draw a table in their notebooks with six lines and two columns. Tell them to write one element on each line. Have them work in pairs and choose a character from page 87 each (Breckinridge 'Renegade' Reed or Serena Seabright). Have pairs go through the text pausing after each element. Tell them to fill in their character information on the table. Have students check with another pair.

Let's talk

- Lead this discussion as some questions are easier to answer than others. For example, help students understand that it is not clear what motivates Reed. Ask them to make suggestions for this themselves using the rest of the description as context.

Language: Participle adjectives page 89

Learning objective

7L7 Use Standard English accurately and at increasing length for a range of topics, purposes and audiences

Activity

- For question 1c, reinforce students' learning by asking: *Which words did you find that are participle adjectives? How do you know? Which words did you find that are verbs? How do you know?*

Vocabulary: Describing appearance and Describing personality pages 90–91

Learning objectives

7SL6 Understand explicit and implicit meaning and details in a range of longer and increasingly complex talk

7L2 Use a wide range of interesting and powerful new words

7L3 Recognise and use a wide range of synonyms and antonyms

Activity 1

- If time allows, you can reinforce vocabulary through a game. Divide the class into two or three teams. Have one volunteer from each team go to the board. Say one of the more interesting adjectives for them to write a sentence using it. Award one point for each correct answer. The team with the most points wins the game.

Activity 2

- As an alternative to questions 1 and 2, you can play 'Positive or Negative?'. Have students make a line in the middle of the classroom or have them stand in their place if there is not enough room available. Write 'Positive' on the left side of the board, and 'Negative' on the right. Explain that you will say one of the more interesting adjectives for them to step to the left or right to indicate if their connotation is positive or negative.

Reading: Character backstories page 92

Learning objective

7R1 Ask and answer a range of questions about longer texts and summarise the main and supporting points

Let's read

- You can remind students about the backstories of the series characters that you shared in the Unit opener. Remind them that not all the information has shown throughout the series but that it can help us understand the characters better.
- Students can make a KWL chart in their notebooks to record what they know, want to know and would like to know about the characters.

Speaking and writing: Writing a backstory page 93

Learning objectives

7SL2 Express ideas, opinions and feelings with increasing detail and clarity, justifying own viewpoint and linking it to others' viewpoints

7SL3 Describe a range of people, places and objects and events in detail using a range of mainly accurate language, choosing interesting language

7SL10 Listen and respond appropriately in a wide range of speaking activities

7SL11 Ask and answer a wide range of questions asking for detailed information and seeking clarification

7W4 Create stories using a range of techniques, e.g. different points of view, creating suspense

Activity

- Suggest students take notes when they are interviewing their partners. Then they can share them with their partners to write the backstory.
- Sharing the character description and backstory with the rest of the class may take a long time. You can have students work in small groups instead.
- Remind students that it is a good idea to start and finish feedback with positive comments about their partner's work. If time allows, students could draw their partner's character and then comment if they are like the author imagined.

Reading and writing: Show, don't tell
page 94

Learning objective
7R5 Explore the language in a wide range of longer Creole and Standard English texts, e.g. poems, stories, age-appropriate novels and non-fiction texts

Let's read
- As students have done similar tasks before, you can give them a minute to read both extracts quickly. Have pairs describe the differences and similarities between the extracts and then answer the Let's talk questions. Ask volunteers why they think the heading of this page is 'Show, don't tell'.

Activity
- If time allows, have pairs create a sentence pair with any of the course characters. Remind them that they should show what the characters are like.

Reading and writing: Introducing a character
page 95

Learning objective
7R4 Explore characters' feelings, personalities and motivations in increasing detail, referring to the text and relating to own experience or other reading

Language and Let's talk
- Ask students to draw a table on their notebooks with six lines and two columns. Tell them to write one characteristic from their Student Book page 88 on each line. Go through the ways of introducing a character and pause after each example (text in green on page 95 of the Student Book). Allow students to complete the table; explain that they may need to interpret some implicit information. Have pairs compare their answers and ask them to work together in Let's talk.
- Check answers as a class and encourage students to reflect on how authors build a character.

Language: Direct speech
page 96

Learning objective
7R5 Explore the language in a wide range of longer Creole and Standard English texts, e.g. poems, stories, age-appropriate novels and non-fiction texts

Activity
- The aim is to get students to articulate their knowledge and misconceptions of how to punctuate direct speech. Make sure you check as a class to discuss understanding and misconceptions.

- If time allows, you can ask students to play with the Language activity examples and change their order and punctuation in a different way, allowing them to add variations. For example: *"Seems to be warming up out there," said the cashier* can turn into: *The cashier said enthusiastically, "Seems to be warming up out there!"* More confident students can try to change the examples in the other two ways of using direct speech.

Reading and writing: What other characters think
page 97

Learning objectives
7R4 Explore characters' feelings, personalities and motivations in increasing detail, referring to the text and relating to own experience or other reading

7W4 Create stories using a range of techniques, e.g. different points of view, creating suspense

Activity
- Before students write their dialogue, ask them to work in pairs. Have them discuss their characters' features and encourage them to ask questions to help their partners to define them better. For example: *Where did the characters meet? Why are they happy/sad/worried? What will happen if ... ? What can you say to imply that ... ?* and so on.

Reading and writing: Challenging your character
page 98

Learning objectives
7R4 Explore characters' feelings, personalities and motivations in increasing detail, referring to the text and relating to own experience or other reading

7W4 Create stories using a range of techniques, e.g. different points of view, creating suspense

Activity
- It is easier for students to develop a story if they do it step by step. As they will be asked to write the start of a story next lesson, you can ask students to develop the plot outline using the dialogue and character design they did on page 97. Allow students to check what they have learned in previous lessons so that they can improve any aspects that needed more work.
- Explain to students that feedback is not only for a final version of a story. Encourage them to work in pairs or small groups. Ask them to share their dialogues and plot outlines. Encourage students to say what they think works or might need extra thought in their partner's work.

Writing: Character storywriting page 99

Learning objectives

7W1 Spell most words correctly and proofread own and others' work for accuracy

7W3 Plan and develop creative writing in a range of different genres of fiction, non-fiction and types of poem, using the most appropriate planning method

7W4 Create stories using a range of techniques, e.g. different points of view, creating suspense

7W7 Evaluate own and others' writing, suggesting improvements including making the writing more powerful and evaluating literary devices

7W8 Write legibly and with appropriate speed and fluency

7W9 Write longer texts, grouping ideas in paragraphs and with an opening and a conclusion

Activity

- Students can use the Character story planner on Workbook page 62 to outline their main character better (this is also on page 64 of this Teacher's Guide).
- Suggest using the Character story techniques checklist as a guide while writing their first draft. Remind them to make sure their handwriting is legible. Encourage them to check this draft for spelling, punctuation, vocabulary or grammar mistakes.
- Allow them to write a second draft for a partner to check. Encourage them to leave enough space between lines to allow partners to add notes, like the sample in 4a. Ask students to pair up with a student they have not worked with recently so that the story is new to them.
- Remind students that they need to check their feedback and assess their partner's suggestions. Monitor and help as necessary. Have students write their final version on a separate piece of paper that you can use to create a Class Storybook.

Projects pages 100–101

Project 1: Performance

Learning objectives

7SL10 Listen and respond appropriately in a wide range of speaking activities

7SL11 Ask and answer a wide range of questions asking for detailed information and seeking clarification

7SL13 Take part in group discussions and problem-solving activities and extended projects, working together to achieve an outcome

Project guidance

- If time allows, both projects can be completed in one session or in several sessions throughout the unit. You may prefer to ask some students to complete Project 1 only.
- If some students are working more than other group members, you can reassign the roles or tasks.
- Less confident students may benefit from having a checklist of features to improve their performance. You can create very simple guidelines with four or five points to bear in mind.
- Before students start working on the project, ask them to refer to their previous Project reflection notes. Tell them to think about what they can do better this time; they can choose just one aspect to improve so that it is more manageable. Encourage students to add feedback to these notes about this performance after Reflection.
- You may want to ask students to prepare their character information in advance. They can also think of some questions their partners might ask and prepare answers that do not reveal their character so easily.

Project 2: Writing

Learning objectives

7SL13 Take part in group discussions and problem-solving activities and extended projects, working together to achieve an outcome

7W3 Plan and develop creative writing in a range of different genres of fiction, non-fiction and types of poem, using the most appropriate planning method

7W5 Write a range of non-fiction text types for different audiences and purposes using appropriate features and adapting language for different audiences

7W7 Evaluate own and others' writing, suggesting improvements including making the writing more powerful and evaluating literary devices

- Students can recycle characters they created in previous lessons. Explain that this can be done only if it makes sense for the characters to be part of the same story.
- You may want to keep developing peer-correction by encouraging students to check the characters' descriptions before displaying them.
- Facilitate the character display according to resources. It would be good to have a variety of media used, but restrict them to 2D portrait pictures, rather than model-making.
- If possible, ask other classes to visit the display and help them to understand the meaning of the descriptions. Encourage the visitors to share ideas for stories that feature the pairs of characters. This will inspire some imaginative thinking and also be lovely feedback.

7 Exploring food

Unit opener
page 104

Learning objectives

7SL1 Speak with confidence, fluency and accurate pronunciation on a wide range of familiar and unfamiliar topics

7SL2 Express ideas, opinions and feelings with increasing detail and clarity, justifying own viewpoint and linking it to others' viewpoints

7SL3 Describe a range of people, places and objects and events in detail using a range of mainly accurate language, choosing interesting language

7SL4 Speak freely, fluently and confidently and at increasing length in Creole and Standard English

7SL5 Use Creole and different registers of Standard English appropriately in a wide range of different contexts to express a wide range of feelings and ideas

7SL12 Take turns when speaking in a range of longer, more complex exchanges, keeping the conversation going, and concluding it effectively

Images and Let's talk

- Use the pictures and the Let's talk questions as a way to gauge students' prior knowledge on the topic, to determine how much detail you can go into, or whether further information is needed to introduce the topic.
- Ask students what their favourite food is. Encourage volunteers to name the most uncommon food they have ever eaten and share their experience of eating it. Have students name foods they eat regularly and write some on the board. Ask pairs to analyse the food on the board and classify it into *Food good for your body* and *Food to eat as a treat*.
- Please note that it is not a good idea to label food as *junk* or *bad*. This can create an emotional response to both crave it and fear it. Students could feel guilty or embarrassed when they eat it. It is best to emphasise the concept of food that we eat as a treat and, therefore, not so often.

Reading: The new school menu
page 105

Learning objectives

7SL7 Read aloud fluently and confidently, with appropriate expression, in a wide range of longer texts

7R4 Explore characters' feelings, personalities and motivations in increasing detail, referring to the text and relating to own experience or other reading

Let's read

- Ask students to scan the text and count how many characters there are in the story and their names. Encourage volunteers to summarise the story.

Activity

- Suggest students look for clues in the text about how a character is speaking, such as adverbs, ellipses or exclamation marks.

Reading: The new school menu (continued)
page 106

Learning objectives

7SL7 Read aloud fluently and confidently, with appropriate expression, in a wide range of longer texts

7R1 Ask and answer a range of questions about longer texts and summarise the main and supporting points

Let's read

- Ask students to read the text aloud in the same groups as in the Activity in the previous lesson. Tell them to keep the character they acted out. They can keep working together to answer the Let's talk questions.

Speaking and listening: Attitudes to food
page 107

Learning objectives

7SL1 Speak with confidence, fluency and accurate pronunciation on a wide range of familiar and unfamiliar topics

7SL2 Express ideas, opinions and feelings with increasing detail and clarity, justifying own viewpoint and linking it to others' viewpoints

7SL11 Ask and answer a wide range of questions asking for detailed information and seeking clarification

7SL12 Take turns when speaking in a range of longer, more complex exchanges, keeping the conversation going, and concluding it effectively

7SL13 Take part in group discussions and problem-solving activities and extended projects, working together to achieve an outcome

Activity

- For the Pair discussion, go through the Speaking skills and Listening skills suggestions. Ask for useful phrases where appropriate and write them on the board. You can do a quick demonstration with a volunteer and pause it to help students notice which suggestions you are showing.
- Ask students what they can do to remember what their partners say. Explain that it is OK to take notes but that they should be brief. Suggest using isolated words only; the objective would be to use the words as prompts rather than record the exact phrases.
- For the Class sharing, use your discretion to facilitate this stage as it can be challenging. Use questions and prompts to support. For example, allow partners to quickly remind the speaker of something they said. If necessary, demonstrate with a volunteer how open questions work better than closed questions.

Language: Phrasal verbs page 108

Learning objectives

7SL10 Listen and respond appropriately in a wide range of speaking activities

7L1 Use a wide range of language forms appropriately

Language and Activity

- For simplicity, the Student Book uses the term *phrasal verbs* rather than *prepositional verbs*.
- Remind students that phrasal verbs are often less formal than a single verb that means the same. For example, *sort out* is less formal than *solve*. Also, phrasal verbs are more common in spoken language.
- Have some dictionaries available and encourage students to use them as necessary.
- You can make a poster with the particles and all the phrasal verbs the students know as a class. Keep it on display for the rest of the unit. Whenever you need to change the class pace, ask a student to choose one phrasal verb. Encourage volunteers to say example sentences.

Vocabulary: Silent letters and unstressed vowels page 109

Learning objectives

7W1 Spell most words correctly and proofread own and others' work for accuracy

7W2 Develop strategies including using known spelling patterns to predict spelling of new words

Language

- Help students remember the patterns. Make sets of cards with one of the patterns and example words on each. Distribute one set to every small group and let them match the patterns with the corresponding words. More confident students may want to add example words to the patterns. Optionally, you can create just one poster with the listed patterns and the example words on a card each. Have volunteers take one word card to match with the corresponding pattern.

Reading: Balanced arguments pages 110–111

Learning objectives

7R1 Ask and answer a range of questions about longer texts and summarise the main and supporting points

7R3 Understand the purpose of different parts of a text in a wide range of texts, including genres of fiction

Let's read

- Draw a table on the board with the headings *Traditional food* and *Modern food*. Add the subheadings *Pros* and *Cons* under each. Check or teach what *Pros* and *Cons* mean. Have students copy the table into their notebooks.
- Ask students to complete the table with notes (main words or prompts, not full ideas) as they read the text. Allow them to use their tables to answer the Let's talk questions.
- Ask pairs to analyse their table and assess how balanced the text is. Encourage them to support their answers. Check as a class.

Reading and writing: Structure and features of a balanced argument page 112

Learning objectives

7R3 Understand the purpose of different parts of a text in a wide range of texts, including genres of fiction

7R5 Explore the language in a wide range of longer Creole and Standard English texts, e.g. poems, stories, age-appropriate novels and non-fiction texts

7L6 Use a range of structural features for effect, e.g. dramatic effect, suspense

Let's talk

- For question 3, you can have students work in small groups to make a Memory game set. Give out 14 cards to each group. Ask them to write the seven language features and the corresponding explanations (with examples) on the cards, with one feature or explanation per card to make a full set. Collect and shuffle each set. Hand out one set to each group, making sure they do not get the set they made. Have students place the cards face down. Tell them to take turns turning up two cards. If they match the explanation with the feature, they keep the pair and get another turn. If they do not find a matching pair, they turn the cards face down again. The student with the most pairs wins the game.

Language: Impersonal voice and quantifiers   page 113

Learning objectives

7L1 Use a wide range of language forms appropriately

7L7 Use Standard English accurately and at increasing length for a range of topics, purposes and audiences

Activity and Language

- For question 1 you may want to guide students more and use these questions instead:
  What examples of impersonal phrases used for introducing ideas did you find?
  What are some examples of ones used for reinforcing ideas?
  What are some examples of ones used for contrasting ideas?
  You can write these questions on the board for students to answer one at a time and then check in pairs.
- As all the sentences in question 2 are facts, facilitate discussion in pairs and then as a class before revealing the answer.

Language and speaking: Connectives in balanced arguments   page 114

Learning objectives

7SL2 Express ideas, opinions and feelings with increasing detail and clarity, justifying own viewpoint and linking it to others' viewpoints

7SL12 Take turns when speaking in a range of longer, more complex exchanges, keeping the conversation going, and concluding it effectively

7L6 Use a range of structural features for effect, e.g. dramatic effect, suspense

7L7 Use Standard English accurately and at increasing length for a range of topics, purposes and audiences

Activity

- For question 2, model the exchange with a volunteer using a topic not listed. For example, for and against the idea that children should spend more time at school every day. Allow students to refer to the Language table during the discussion. You can challenge more confident students by asking them to make sure they include one connective of each type in their argument.

Language: Colons and semi-colons   page 115

Learning objectives

7W11 Use a wide range of punctuation appropriately

7L7 Use Standard English accurately and at increasing length for a range of topics, purposes and audiences

Activity

- It may be a good idea to make a Punctuation poster with all the marks in question 1. Elicit their names and add an example or two for each. Students can copy it into their notebooks to use as reference whenever they are practising their writing skills.

Listening and speaking: New food   page 116

Learning objectives

7SL2 Express ideas, opinions and feelings with increasing detail and clarity, justifying own viewpoint and linking it to others' viewpoints

7SL3 Describe a range of people, places and objects and events in detail using a range of mainly accurate language, choosing interesting language

7SL4 Speak freely, fluently and confidently and at increasing length in Creole and Standard English

7SL12 Take turns when speaking in a range of longer, more complex exchanges, keeping the conversation going, and concluding it effectively

Let's talk

- Advise students to take notes of their discussion as they can be used in the next lesson to write a balanced argument. Remind them that taking notes is just writing some words as a reminder of the points discussed. Elicit why it is not a good idea to take detailed notes (we might focus on the writing and stop listening to our partners).
- Write *For* and *Against* on the board. Discuss question 4 as a class and take notes on the board accordingly.

Writing: Writing a balanced argument
page 117

Learning objectives

7W5 Write a range of non-fiction text types for different audiences and purposes using appropriate features and adapting language for different audiences

7W7 Evaluate own and others' writing, suggesting improvements including making the writing more powerful and evaluating literary devices

7W9 Write longer texts, grouping ideas in paragraphs and with an opening and a conclusion

Activity

- Write the title *Should we try new food?* on the board. Elicit arguments for and against it.
- Students can use the Balanced argument planner on Workbook page 72 to make sure they have enough for and against arguments (this is also on page 65 of this Teacher's Guide). The planner also helps students to make sure they have all the necessary elements to write a successful balanced argument.
- Suggest using the Balanced argument checklist as a guide while writing their first draft. Remind students to make sure their handwriting is legible. Encourage them to check this draft for spelling, punctuation, vocabulary or grammar mistakes. Explain that as they are writing two drafts and a final version of their argument, they need to write with appropriate speed and fluency.
- Allow them to write a second draft for a partner to check, encouraging them to leave enough space between lines to allow partners to add notes. Ask students to pair up with a student they have not worked with recently so that they are not biased.
- Remind students that they need to check the feedback and assess their partner's suggestions. Ask: *Are your partner's comments contributing to improving your work? Will their suggestions help with the flow of your argument?* Monitor and help as necessary.

Projects
pages 118–119

Project 1: Writing

Learning objectives

7SL9 Plan and deliver a presentation, adapting the content and language to the audience

7SL13 Take part in group discussions and problem-solving activities and extended projects, working together to achieve an outcome

7W5 Write a range of non-fiction text types for different audiences and purposes using appropriate features and adapting language for different audiences

7W7 Evaluate own and others' writing, suggesting improvements including making the writing more powerful and evaluating literary devices

Project guidance

- If time allows, both projects can be completed in one session or in several sessions throughout the unit. You may prefer to choose one project for students to complete. Alternatively, you may wish to give students the choice of which project they would like to complete.
- If some students are working more than other group members, you can reassign the roles or tasks.
- Ask students to research the basic features for a successful poster, booklet or digital presentation based on their choice for the fact file.

Project 2: Debate

Learning objectives

7SL2 Express ideas, opinions and feelings with increasing detail and clarity, justifying own viewpoint and linking it to others' viewpoints

7SL4 Speak freely, fluently and confidently and at increasing length in Creole and Standard English

7SL10 Listen and respond appropriately in a wide range of speaking activities

7SL13 Take part in group discussions and problem-solving activities and extended projects, working together to achieve an outcome

- You may need to make sure that there is a similar number of groups proposing and opposing the motion.
- Monitor and, if necessary, give further guidance on how to prepare materials for the debate. Go through the Debate dos and don'ts checklist before the debate as a reminder.
- Read the motion aloud to start the debate, as you will act as the moderator.
- Before moving on to step 6, you may wish to open the floor to give students an opportunity to express their points, opinions and facts and ask any questions or queries. Anyone may now speak, either for or against the motion. This can put students' persuasive skills to the test in a spontaneous way.
- Decide how the vote should be cast, publicly or by secret ballot, based on how the debate went.
- Less confident students may benefit from having a checklist of features to improve their performance. You can create very simple guidelines with four or five points to bear in mind.
- Before students start working on the project, ask them to refer to their previous Project reflection notes. Tell them to think about what they can do better this time. Encourage them to add feedback to these notes about this performance after Reflection.

Moving on

Unit opener
page 120

Learning objectives

7SL1 Speak with confidence, fluency and accurate pronunciation on a wide range of familiar and unfamiliar topics

7SL2 Express ideas, opinions and feelings with increasing detail and clarity, justifying own viewpoint and linking it to others' viewpoints

7SL3 Describe a range of people, places and objects and events in detail using a range of mainly accurate language, choosing interesting language

7SL4 Speak freely, fluently and confidently and at increasing length in Creole and Standard English

7SL5 Use Creole and different registers of Standard English appropriately in a wide range of different contexts to express a wide range of feelings and ideas

7SL12 Take turns when speaking in a range of longer, more complex exchanges, keeping the conversation going, and concluding it effectively

Images and Let's talk

- Use the pictures and the Let's talk questions as a way to gauge students' prior knowledge on the topic, to determine how much detail you can go into, or whether further information is needed to introduce the topic.

- Ask pairs to take turns describing the pictures. Encourage them to speculate about each situation. For example: *The two men are interviewing the young man for a new job. He's finished his degree. His hands show he is nervous but he is a very good candidate.*

- Some students may feel uneasy about starting a new school cycle. Help them remember how they felt when they started primary school and how many great experiences they have had since then.

- If appropriate, elicit ways to help students embrace change. Ask what they have done in the past when they lived through a big change. Tell them that they can also talk to their parents or guardians about how they feel and ask for advice.

Reading: Looking back and looking forward
page 121

Learning objectives

7SL2 Express ideas, opinions and feelings with increasing detail and clarity, justifying own viewpoint and linking it to others' viewpoints

7SL4 Speak freely, fluently and confidently and at increasing length in Creole and Standard English

7R4 Explore characters' feelings, personalities and motivations in increasing detail, referring to the text and relating to own experience or other reading

7R8 Read age-appropriate texts fluently and with understanding

Let's read

- Have students read the text and find information they didn't know or didn't remember about the characters. Then ask them to write three words that describe each character. Have pairs compare their words and then answer the Let's talk questions.

Reading: Poems that look back to the past
page 122

Learning objectives

7SL7 Read aloud fluently and confidently, with appropriate expression, in a wide range of longer texts

7SL12 Take turns when speaking in a range of longer, more complex exchanges, keeping the conversation going, and concluding it effectively

7R7 Talk about stories and poems they like in detail and give reasons, referring to the text

Let's read and Let's talk

- Ask students who the poet is and if they have heard of him. If necessary, tell them that James Berry was born in Jamaica in 1924, where he grew up in a farming family in a small seaside village. Ask volunteers if they have anything in common with the poet.

- Have pairs read the poem aloud, taking turns. Although the Student Book suggests switching after every sentence, you may wish to change the length. More confident students may work better changing turns after they finish a stanza.

- When students share their ideas with the class, prompt them to go back to the lines of the poem to support their answers. Suggest saying the stanza number first and then the corresponding line number.

Reading: Poems that look back to the past (continued) page 123

Learning objectives

7SL7 Read aloud fluently and confidently, with appropriate expression, in a wide range of longer texts

7R1 Ask and answer a range of questions about longer texts and summarise the main and supporting points

7R7 Talk about stories and poems they like in detail and give reasons, referring to the text

Let's talk

- Optionally, you can ask pairs to choose a poem each and answer questions 2 or 3 and 4 only. Tell them to share their answers and then switch poems to check if they agree with their partner's point of view. Have them answer the rest of the questions.
- Have volunteers go to the board to write all the poetic devices they remember. Go through them and add any others they might have missed. Ask students which poem from pages 122–123 they liked the most and group them accordingly. Tell them to analyse the poem and share their findings with the rest of the class.

Language: Oxymorons and Symbolism pages 124–125

Learning objectives

7SL3 Describe a range of people, places and objects and events in detail using a range of mainly accurate language, choosing interesting language

7R6 Explore a range of literary features and discuss writers' intentions, beginning to give support from the text

Activity 1

- If suitable, you can also discuss as a class how *terribly good* and *whole piece* are also oxymorons.

Activity 2

- To round up the lessons, you can ask students to create a character and assign a name, a symbol and an oxymoron to describe them. If time allows, they can also draw a picture. Display the work and have students choose their three favourites. Ask volunteers to share their choice and encourage them to support their answer.

Speaking and listening: Memories from school page 126

Learning objectives

7SL3 Describe a range of people, places and objects and events in detail using a range of mainly accurate language, choosing interesting language

7SL11 Ask and answer a wide range of questions asking for detailed information and seeking clarification

7SL12 Take turns when speaking in a range of longer, more complex exchanges, keeping the conversation going, and concluding it effectively

7SL13 Take part in group discussions and problem-solving activities and extended projects, working together to achieve an outcome

Activity

- Go through the 'Show you are listening by' tips before students sit in a circle. You may ask why each suggestion helps you focus on what you are listening to.
- Ask students not to repeat questions. Optionally, you can allow speakers to choose their question.
- Tell groups to make sure that each speaker is asked at least one question to get more information.
- If time allows, have students draw one of their group members doing an action related to the memory they shared. It might be easier to assign this task to the student to their right. When students get their drawing, they can write a caption summarising the memory. Display the work.

Writing: School memories poem page 127

Learning objectives

7W3 Plan and develop creative writing in a range of different genres of fiction, non-fiction and types of poem, using the most appropriate planning method

7W6 Write a range of literary texts of increasing length, e.g. stories, poems and scripts using literary devices studied so far for effect

7W7 Evaluate own and others' writing, suggesting improvements including making the writing more powerful and evaluating literary devices

7W10 Use appropriate layout when writing a wide range of longer texts, e.g. stories, poems, information texts, presentations, scripts

Activity

- Students can use the School memories poem planner on Workbook page 79 (this is also on page 66 of this Teacher's Guide). This planner offers an alternative way to organise the poem.

- Remind students to make sure their handwriting is legible. Encourage them to check their first draft for spelling, punctuation, vocabulary or grammar mistakes. Explain that as they are writing two drafts and a final version of their poem, they need to write with appropriate speed and fluency. Tell them to leave enough space between lines when they write the second draft so that partners have room for notes or feedback.
- Collect poems and shuffle them. As you hand them out, make sure students do not get their own poem.
- Ask students to write their final version on a separate piece of paper. Collect them and make a School Memories Poetry Book.

Reading: A letter to my future self
page 128

Learning objectives

7R4 Explore characters' feelings, personalities and motivations in increasing detail, referring to the text and relating to own experience or other reading

7R5 Explore the language in a wide range of longer Creole and Standard English texts, e.g. poems, stories, age-appropriate novels and non-fiction texts

7R8 Read age-appropriate texts fluently and with understanding

Let's read

- You may need to go through basic information about letters before working on the Student Book. Ask students if they have ever received a letter. If they have, encourage them to share their experience with the rest of the class and say why they got it, how they felt and if they replied to it. If they have not, you may have to explain that in the past, before the internet and email services were available, people used letters to communicate when they were not near each other. The letters would be sent to the recipient in an envelope via the mail service.
- Write these questions on the board for students to analyse Omar's letter as they read it:
  Address — business or private?
  Greeting — formal or informal?
  Style of letter — friendly or business?
  What is the message?
  How does the letter end?
  Have pairs share their answers.
- If suitable, you can go back to the letter and expand the lesson. Here are some features of letters:
  Sender's address – on the top right-hand corner of the page; include telephone number and email if available
  Greeting – choose depending on how well you know the person: Dear Maya, Hi Kwame, Greetings
  Complimentary close — short comment; for example, Love, Lots of love, With thanks, See you soon, Kind regards, Yours sincerely.

Speaking and listening: Aspirations
page 129

Learning objectives

7SL2 Express ideas, opinions and feelings with increasing detail and clarity, justifying own viewpoint and linking it to others' viewpoints

7SL4 Speak freely, fluently and confidently and at increasing length in Creole and Standard English

7SL12 Take turns when speaking in a range of longer, more complex exchanges, keeping the conversation going, and concluding it effectively

Activity

- Before you start the game, write *Aspirations* on the board. Ask students to go back to page 121 and find the aspirations of each character. Then ask volunteers to share their own aspirations. It might be helpful to model the game before pair work begins.

Let's talk

- Lead the activity, encouraging students to articulate their motivations and values and give reasons for their choices. You could ask students to prepare something in writing before posing these questions and to allow their partners to ask questions.
- Remind students that their aspirations are often linked to their values. For example, if you value risk-taking and adventure, you are more likely to want to start your own business or to go into Space!

Language: Punctuating a letter
page 130

Learning objectives

7W11 Use a wide range of punctuation appropriately

7L7 Use Standard English accurately and at increasing length for a range of topics, purposes and audiences

Language

- Activate students' prior knowledge and elicit general rules for using commas and capital letters. Take notes in the board. Ask if students know any special conventions when writing letters. Go through the text in the Student Book and complement the board notes adding a *Letters* section. Ask students to copy them into their notebooks. Optionally, they can add notes about other punctuation marks when working on the Activity. Assess this work to plan any necessary revision work.

Language: Commas: A revision page 131

Learning objectives

7W11 Use a wide range of punctuation appropriately

7L1 Use a wide range of language forms appropriately

Language

- Ask students to compare the information that they wrote about commas in their notebooks in the previous lesson with the text in the Student Book. Have them add any information they might have missed. If time allows, encourage them to add examples of their own. This can also be done in small groups or pairs.

Language: Types of compound words page 132

Learning objectives

7W1 Spell most words correctly and proofread own and others' work for accuracy

7W2 Develop strategies including using known spelling patterns to predict spelling of new words

7W11 Use a wide range of punctuation appropriately

Language

- Have small groups work together to write a definition of compound words. Check answers as a class.
- Challenge groups to write as many compound words as they can within two minutes.
- Ask them to go through the text in the Student Book and classify their words into closed, open and hyphenated. Monitor their work and help as necessary.

Tip

- Make sure that students understand that blended words are not compound words; you could use false statements for them to correct.
- Share some other examples: *smog*: smoke and fog; *internet*: interconnected and network; *podcast*: iPod and broadcast; *vlog*: video and log.

Writing: Write a letter to your future self page 133

Learning objectives

7W3 Plan and develop creative writing in a range of different genres of fiction, non-fiction and types of poem, using the most appropriate planning method

7W8 Write legibly and with appropriate speed and fluency

7W10 Use appropriate layout when writing a wide range of longer texts, e.g. stories, poems, information texts, presentations, scripts

7W11 Use a wide range of punctuation appropriately

Activity

- Tell students to go through the previous work on their personal aspirations from page 129. Ask them to read what they are expected to discuss in question 1 and prepare some notes.
- Encourage students to use the Letter writing checklist as they plan their letter. They can also use the letter features they recorded when working on page 128. Explain that as this is a personal work, their letter will not be checked by a partner but that it's always good to check our own work.
- Encourage students to check their first draft as they have throughout the school year: check content, and also check for any spelling, punctuation, vocabulary and grammar mistakes. As they write their final version, remind them to make sure their handwriting is legible. If time allows, they can decorate and illustrate their letter either by drawing or gluing cut-outs from magazines.
- Help students to think how long they want to wait until they open their letter. Ask: *When would be a good time to read it? After you finish a certain education level, like high school or university, or a milestone birthday?*
- You can also help students to consider how to keep their letter safely. Ask: *Will you keep it in a drawer, or inside a book? Can you give it to a person you trust to keep it safe? Will you put it into a container and bury it? Any other ideas?*

Projects

pages 134–135

Project 1: Performance

Learning objectives

7SL7 Read aloud fluently and confidently, with appropriate expression, in a wide range of longer texts

7SL13 Take part in group discussions and problem-solving activities and extended projects, working together to achieve an outcome

7W5 Write a range of non-fiction text types for different audiences and purposes using appropriate features and adapting language for different audiences

7W10 Use appropriate layout when writing a wide range of longer texts, e.g. stories, poems, information texts, presentations, scripts

Project guidance

- If time allows, both projects can be completed in one session or in several sessions throughout the unit. You may prefer to choose one project for students to complete. Alternatively, you may wish to give students the choice of which project they would like to complete.
- If some students are working more than other group members, you can reassign the roles or tasks.
- Less confident students may benefit from having a checklist of features to improve their performance. You can create very simple guidelines with four or five points to bear in mind.
- Before students start working on the project, ask them to refer to their previous Project reflection notes. Tell them to think about what they can do better this time; they can choose just one aspect to improve so that it is more manageable. After Reflection, encourage students to record how they have improved their work throughout the nine units.
- Lead step 2 as you will have to decide on the logistics of where and when the performance will take place, and who will be invited. For example, it could be a special assembly, or it could be an open class for parents and guardians.
- Groups will also need your help to find suitable physical locations and/or distributing the adverts more widely in newsletters or digital methods, such as a school website.

Project 2: Writing

Learning objectives

7SL13 Take part in group discussions and problem-solving activities and extended projects, working together to achieve an outcome

7W5 Write a range of non-fiction text types for different audiences and purposes using appropriate features and adapting language for different audiences

7W7 Evaluate own and others' writing, suggesting improvements including making the writing more powerful and evaluating literary devices

7W8 Write legibly and with appropriate speed and fluency

Project guidance

- Organise step 2 in conjunction with the teacher(s) of younger classes. Passing on their expert knowledge to younger students is a worthwhile activity that leavers really enjoy, and is a lovely pastoral activity too.

9 Preparing for tests

Let's talk

- Introduce the topic of the end of year tests.
- Read, or ask a student to read, the Let's talk questions. Give time for discussion in pairs each time.
- Move around the pairs, listening and asking follow-up questions.
- Encourage follow-up discussion. This is a good opportunity to deal with queries or fears and to emphasise the positive aspects of the tests, for example, tests give students an opportunity to show what they can do, tests only test what students have covered in class, and that tests are not to be feared but are just a part of life.

Reading: Let's prepare for a test   pages 137–138

Activity (page 137)

- Students can work individually to read the text 'Tips for test success' silently and write their answers to the questions.
- Alternatively, students can work in pairs to discuss the questions before writing their answers.

Let's talk (page 138)

- Ask students to read the text 'During the test' silently. Support less confident students by asking questions to check understanding while they are reading.
- Check understanding of the whole class of the terms, such as *multiple-choice questions*.
- Students can work in pairs or groups of three to discuss the answers to the questions.
- For question 6, allow sufficient time for students to discuss this in detail and share their ideas.
- Take feedback and write good ideas on the board for students to use in the next activity.

Activity (page 138)

- Check that students understand what they are going to do.
- Elicit features of an advice text. These might include the language needed for giving advice, such as, *It's a good idea to ... you should ... don't forget to ... it's important to ... remember to ...*
- Students can make their checklist in groups or pairs, but should write their texts individually. This will give you valuable feedback on their writing skills.
- Encourage students to share their finished writing with a partner and give each other feedback, using the questions in point 4.

Speaking and reading: Study tips   pages 139–140

Let's talk (page 139)

- As students read the characters' questions, encourage them to share whether they have similar questions or concerns.
- Allow time for pairs to discuss possible solutions to the questions. They could share with another pair before sharing with the class if time allows, to allow them to decide on the best solutions.

Let's talk (page 140)

- Students can read the study tips silently, or in pairs, taking turns to read a paragraph each. If students read aloud, this allows for discussion of each point during the reading activity.
- Encourage students to discuss their answers to the questions. Take note of any differences in their responses, and you may wish to develop these into a discussion.
- For question 2, students can make a list of words each, or you can make a class list on the board, based on their suggestions, adding any words you know they need to revise. They can make flashcards in class or for homework.
- You may wish to develop the idea of mind maps from the text and students could make mind maps of different concepts for revision, for example, literary devices with examples, verb forms with examples, interesting and powerful adjectives, synonyms and antonyms.

Language   page 141

Activities

- The activities on this page provide revision and preparation for the test-style practice questions on the following pages. Students are encouraged to complete the activities in pairs to build confidence for the test-style practice questions. Confident students may wish to complete the activities individually.
- For extension of Activities 2 and 3, students can put each word into a sentence of their own to check they are using the word correctly.

Test-style practice questions   pages 142–149

These pages provide practice in the main question types students are likely to encounter in the test. The wording of each question may not exactly match what they will see on their test paper, but the range of questions cover those found in the different PLA test papers.

- It would be a good idea to do one question together in each section to build confidence.
- Students can use these questions for test practice under timed conditions.
- Students can mark each other's work to ensure that they do not change their answers during the marking.
- Use the students' answers to plan revision activities to focus on the areas where students may still need support.

Reading and speaking: Review your reading skills   page 150

Let's talk
- Students work in pairs or small groups to assess their own reading skills and revision needs.
- Use their responses to the questions to plan revision activities.

Activity
- Questions 3–7 provide activities that will support students in their revision of reading skills. Allow sufficient time for each activity to help provide effective revision classes.

Speaking and writing: Brush up your writing skills   page 151

Activities
- The first activity provides revision of what is needed for all the different text types that students have covered. They can look back in their Student Book to help them.
- The revision leads into practice test-type writing tasks. Some of these should be done individually under timed conditions, but some could be done as a classroom activity with discussion to build confidence. Students can plan the task in pairs, then produce either one written text each, or one between two for less confident students.

Writing assessment grid

The writing assessment grid on the following page can be used when marking any test-type writing task. The assessment objectives are based on the Oxford pan-Caribbean PLA Programme of Study learning objectives, which are in turn based on the combined learning objectives of all the Caribbean PLA curricula.

Individual test writing assessment grids may differ slightly from this one in wording or layout. However, the assessment objectives will test the same skills. Grids may be read across from left to right, or vertically from top to bottom (or bottom to top). This one is designed to be read from top to bottom.

The total number of marks available for a test-type writing task using this marking grid is 20. This may be different from the total number of marks allocated for writing in your PLA exit test. You will see that the writing assessment grid is designed so that fewer marks are allocated to *Vocabulary* and *Spelling*, and more marks are allocated to *Structure and organisation* and *Grammar and punctuation*. This is called *weighting*. It gives more importance in the assessment to *Structure and organisation* and *Grammar and punctuation* than to *Vocabulary* and *Spelling*. Your individual writing assessment objectives may or may not be 'weighted' like this.

How to use the writing assessment grid

The assessment grid is primarily for use by teachers, with test-type writing tasks for students aged 9-11 (*Let's Leap!* Levels 6–7). Use your judgement when deciding whether or not to ask students to use the grid to mark each other's work. It shows them how their own work may be assessed in the test, but can be intimidating, so it may be preferable for them to use the checklists in the Student Books to mark each other's writing.

Things to consider when marking:
- When marking a student's written work (or when students are marking their own work), start at the top of Column 1, Content.
- If the piece of writing does not meet the descriptor(s) in the top row, move down to the next row.
- When the descriptor fits the student's work, award that mark for content.
- Repeat this process for each of the other columns in turn.
- Add the marks together to arrive at the student's mark for that piece of writing. The mark is out of a maximum of 20.

Additional guidance:
- A student's writing may not exactly meet the descriptor in a given category. If this is the case, choose the descriptor that is the 'best fit'.
- Two categories, *Structure and organisation* and *Grammar and punctuation*, contain more than one descriptor in each band. Again, choose the band with the best fit when awarding the mark.

Marks	Content	Vocabulary	Structure and organisation	Grammar and punctuation	Spelling
5			Paragraphs used to group ideas with progression between paragraphs. A range of cohesive features used appropriately and for effect (e.g. dramatic, suspense, argument). Almost all the organisational features of a given text type used appropriately.	A wide range of Standard English used accurately. A wide range of punctuation used appropriately.	
4	Relevant and interesting with extensive details.		Paragraphs used to group ideas with some progression. A range of cohesive devices used appropriately. Most of the organisational features of the required text type used appropriately.	A range of Standard English used mostly accurately. Almost all punctuation used appropriately in an increasing range.	
3	Relevant with some detail.	Use of interesting and powerful vocabulary. Use of language features, e.g. literary devices.	Some use of paragraphs to group ideas. Some use of cohesive devices (e.g. adverbials of time and place to link ideas). Some of the features of the required text type used appropriately.	Standard English used mostly accurately. Most punctuation used appropriately.	Most words spelled correctly, including uncommon and multi-syllabic words.
2	Content is relevant to the task.	Sufficient appropriate vocabulary and language used to meet the basic demands of the task.	Some attempt to organise ideas. Use of simple conjunctions (e.g. and, but, because). Attempt to use some features of the required text type.	Some Standard English structures used accurately. Some punctuation used appropriately.	Most common words spelled correctly, including multi-syllabic words.
1	Some relevant content.	Some vocabulary suitable for the task.	Recognisably an attempt at the required text type (e.g. story/explanation text).	Occasionally accurate use of Standard English. Some correct use of full stops and capital letters.	Some common words spelled correctly.
0	No creditable content.	No creditable content.	No creditable content.	No creditable content.	No creditable content.

Assessment answers

Assessment 1, Units 1–3   pages 52–53

1. a. <u>May</u> I borrow your umbrella to keep dry on the way home?
    b. Perhaps you <u>could</u> help me with the cleaning later.
    c. You <u>shouldn't</u> waste time playing video games in the holidays.
    d. <u>Must</u> we wait for the others to arrive before we eat?
    e. She <u>can</u> play the guitar and she <u>might</u> learn the drums too.   5 marks
2. a. would beat
    b. would have stayed
    c. could have seen
    d. should tell   4 marks
3. Students' own extended sentence using *therefore*, *although* and *as a result of*.   3 marks
4. clichés, technical vocabulary, emphasis   3 marks
5. a. continuous present
    b. present perfect
    c. simple present   3 marks
6. a. The witness stated "I saw the car swerve to miss a cat."
    b. "That work was hard, but I did my best," reported the student.
    c. Our teacher once said "You can do anything you want with determination."
    d. "My coach and I have not fallen out," claimed the tennis player.   4 marks
7. a. The winning goal in the cup final was scored (by my brother).
    b. Her teammates named Shanice Outstanding Player of the Season./Shanice's teammates named her Outstanding Player of the Season.
    c. Each team member was chosen based on their skills and experience (by the manager).
    d. A spectator in the stands caught the cricket ball.   4 marks
8. a. simile
    b. metaphor
    c. personification   3 marks
9. The new restaurant has five-star reviews. It boasts high-quality service and welcomes well-behaved children. Better still, it also has rock-bottom prices. It is perfect for a family get-together!   5 marks
10. Students' own selection of writing task.   12 marks

Common language misconceptions

Some language concepts or grammar rules can be particularly challenging for some students. Below is a list of features covered in the assessments, and page reminders of where guidance is provided to clarify and address any misconceptions:

- Modal verbs of possibility and permission – Student Book, page 8
- Modal verbs of ability, obligation and advice – Student Book, page 14
- Conditional sentences (difference between zero and first conditional) – Student Book, page 15

Assessment 2, Units 4–6 pages 102–103

1. a. At about seven o'clock, tonight's performance will begin.
    b. In the car, the three brothers were arguing about who should sit in the middle.
    c. As fast as she could, the teacher tidied the classroom.   3 marks
2. … start with a promise sentence … ask questions but not give answers … use empty words like *someone*.   3 marks
3. antitoxin, foreground, present, extraordinary, midnight, protest   6 marks
4. a. tone
    b. purpose
    c. audience
    d. form   4 marks
5. a. opinion
    b. opinion
    c. fact
    d. fact   4 marks
6. a. interested
    b. surprised
    c. unsatisfying
    d. boring   3 marks
7. small – squat – lanky
    good – virtuous – immoral
    greedy – avaricious – generous   9 marks
8. "Come and see what I found," said my brother.
    I hesitated before answering, "Why would I trust you, you tricked me last time."
    "That's true," he replied. "But this time it's not a joke."   3 marks
9. Students' own selection of writing task.   12 marks

Common language misconceptions

Some language concepts or grammar rules can be particularly challenging for some students. Below is a list of features covered in the assessments, and page reminders of where guidance is provided to clarify and address any misconceptions:

Adverbials – Student Book, page 59
Less common prefixes – Student Book, page 75
Participle adjectives – Student Book, page 89
Punctuating direct speech – Student Book, page 96

Unit 9: Preparing for tests
pages 142–149

Test-style practice questions, pages 142–149

Spelling, page 142
1. b. achieve   2. a. strict   3. b. friendly

Grammar, pages 142–143
1. c. worse
2. a. would
3. b. most colourful
4. c. was built
5. c. were waiting
6. can't
7. Would
8. did
9. Were
10. Has laid

1. Nouns: holidays, grandma, house, week; Verbs: went, stayed
2. Nouns: books, teacher, page; Verbs: Open, said, turn
3. Nouns: school, bus; Verbs: have to, walk, have missed
4. Nouns: book, characters, adventures; Verbs: love, recommended, said, have
5. Nouns: cricket, exams; Verbs: wish, could, play, sighed, have to, prepare

1. Mr French told the children to stop, look and listen before they crossed the road.
2. Latoya said she couldn't come till later because she had to help her grandma in the garden.
3. The teacher told everyone to take their books and pencils outside as they were having the lesson under the trees.
4. Aidan asked if he could come back tomorrow because he doesn't have any money today.
5. Kwame said that he needed to fix his bike because it's got a puncture.

1. The roofer mended the hole in the roof.
2. The church ladies cleaned the church.
3. The pupils of St Joseph's School performed the play.
4. Priya's mother has grown those beautiful flowers.
5. The children visited the old people and gave them cakes.

Vocabulary, pages 144–145
1. c. relieved
2. a. unique
3. a. disrespectful
4. a. impressive
5. b. likely

1. children
2. women
3. potatoes
4. dresses
5. buses

Answers will vary:
1. definitely
2. quite
3. sure
4. prefer
5. quiet

1. b. interesting
2. a. brave
3. b. ignorant
4. b. artificial
5. a. remembered

Answers will vary:
1. big/huge
2. praised/congratulated
3. brave
4. tiny
5. best

Punctuation and capitalisation, page 146
1. c.   2. c.   3. c.   4. b.   5. c.

1. I haven't seen Maya all week. I think she's on holiday.
2. "What time does the concert start?" asked Aidan.
3. "I don't know. I didn't hear what she said," Kwame replied.
4. "Would you like an ice cream?" "Yes, I would."
5. The boys walked down the long, narrow, sandy path to the beach.

Reading, page 147
1. Students' own sentences. Sentences should include correct grammar and punctuation. (An invasive species is a species of plant or animal that has made its way to places it never lived naturally.)
2. Regrettably
3. Students' own sentences. Sentences should include correct grammar and punctuation. (Climate change and human activity are likely causes of species becoming invasive.)
4. Students' own sentences. Sentences should include correct grammar and punctuation. (The Red Palm Mite and the Giant African Snail are both animals.)

5. Students' own sentences. Sentences should include correct grammar and punctuation. (The Red Palm Mite is a lethal pest found on the areca palm, date palm and coconut. It can attach itself to human objects like bowls and hats, so can travel large distances via tourists; The Giant African Snail can change habitats, eat other snails' food and causes problems for agriculture. It can also spread lethal diseases; Frosty pod rot destroys the inside of cocoa pods and rots the beans and can destroy an entire cocoa crop.)
6. Students' own sentences. Sentences should include correct grammar and punctuation. (The Red Palm Mite can be spread by tourists, as the mites can attach themselves to human objects that then travel to different places along with the tourists.)
7. Students' own titles. (Invasive Species. The Species have Invaded! Invasion of New Species!)

Reading, page 148

1. 'nomad' means the same as 'wanderer'.
2. Students' own sentences. Sentences should include correct grammar and punctuation. (The poet says the river is a 'wanderer' because it wanders through the countryside and doesn't stay still.)
3. Students' own sentences. Sentences should include correct grammar and punctuation. (The poet says the river 'just cannot be still' because the river is always moving.)
4. Students' own sentences. Sentences should include correct grammar and punctuation. (Perhaps the river could hoard human rubbish that has ended up in the river. Also, it could hoard fish, other creatures and plants that live in the river.)
5. Students' own sentences. Sentences should include correct grammar and punctuation. (The poet thinks the river sounds like a baby because it gurgles and hums.)
6. Students' own sentences. Sentences should include correct grammar and punctuation. (The poet means that the river has knocked down some trees or branches with the force of its current or in storms.)
7. b. metaphor
8. gobbled, gurgled
9. Students' own sentences. Sentences should include correct grammar and punctuation. (Yes, I think the poet likes the river because she sounds excited by the river's freedom, versatility and power.)

Reading, page 149

1. Students' own sentences. Sentences should include correct grammar and punctuation. (Miss Myrtle has lived in her town for a long time because everybody knows her.)
2. Students' own sentences. Sentences should include correct grammar and punctuation. (Miss Myrtle is old because she is described as hobbling and she also has a walking stick.)
3. onomatopoeia
4. Students' own sentences. Sentences should include correct grammar and punctuation. (She goes up the hill to feed all the local cats.)
5. Students' own sentences. Sentences should include correct grammar and punctuation. (We know that her bag is heavy because it makes a thump when she puts it down and she has to rub her back.)
6. Students' own sentences. Sentences should include correct grammar and punctuation. (I think she loves the cats because she goes every day to feed them. She also talks to them and strokes them.)
7. Students' own sentences. Sentences should include correct grammar and punctuation. (A simile is used in the first sentence of paragraph 4. This tells us the cats keep appearing and there are lots of them.)
8. 'shimmy' and 'snaking' describe how the cats move.
9. Students' own sentences. Sentences should include correct grammar and punctuation. (The cats are hungry because they're stray cats. They don't have owners/homes.)
10. Students' own sentences. Sentences should include correct grammar and punctuation. (The author uses a short sentence at the end of the extract to build suspense for the next part of the story.)

Assessment 3, Units 7–9   pages 152–153

1. bilder, doutful, arcitect's, brige, new, colums, rong, lisen, couldn't, diffrences, resined, seprate   12 marks
2. title as a question – opening statement – arguments for – arguments against – conclusion
                                                                  5 marks
3. a. personal voice
   b. impersonal voice
   c. personal voice
   d. impersonal voice   4 marks

4. a. His favourite hobbies are: judo, water-colour painting and mountain biking.
   b. The prime minister gave the following answer: "I will do my best for my country."
   c. I had to change my clothes: they were covered in paint.   3 marks
5. living rooms, passers-by, mothers-in-law, honeycombs, get-togethers   5 marks
6. a. Omar opened the door, stepped outside, walked to the gate and waved to Aiden.
   b. Latoya, who loved racing against her friends, bought some new trainers.
   c. Before training, Maya went for something to eat.
   d. Whenever Priya has time, she makes rotis for her family.   4 marks
7. Students' own selection of writing task.   12 marks
8. b. Do something you enjoy
   c. Have a healthy evening meal   2 marks
9. a. had finished, knocked
   b. Have, washed
   c. will go   4 marks
10.a. The woman asked [politely] where the bus stop was.
   b. Priya said she couldn't come to the park because she was [they were] going to visit her aunties.
   c. The head teacher announced that the winning team would win the School Football Cup. 3 marks

Common language misconceptions

Some language concepts or grammar rules can be particularly challenging for some students. Below is a list of features covered in the assessments, and page reminders of where guidance is provided to clarify and address any misconceptions:

Impersonal voice – Student Book, page 113

Colons – Student Book, page 115

Commas – revision – Student Book, page 131

For guidance on marking test-type writing tasks (question 9 on page 103 and question 7 on page 153), please see page 42 of this Teacher's Guide.

Workbook answer key

Unit 1 Beyond Earth

Caribbean astronauts, pages 4–5

1. Students' own words.
2. Students' own answers.
3. VSS Unity 25
4. a. 50,000 feet
   b. 55 miles above the Earth
5. Antigua and Barbuda
6. Hanover
7. Students' own answers.
8. standard
9. Students' own summaries.

Would you go to space?, page 6

Students' own paragraph.

Modal verbs of possibility and permission, page 7

1. Students circle: can, could, may, might
2. a. According to the forecast, there (might) be a storm tomorrow.
   b. (Can) it really be time to go home already?
   c. (May) I please eat the last slice of cake?
   d. We (could) have good news for you tomorrow.
3. a. May I swim here? – Am I allowed to swim here?
   b. The town could be cut off by floods. – The town might be cut off by the floods.
4. a. You can't/cannot choose what to do tonight.
   b. She might not tell you the truth.
   c. Couldn't I/Could I not borrow your pencil quickly?
5. a. He might have sent you an email.
   b. She may have become a professional tennis player.
   c. Things could have been so different.

Extending sentences, page 8

1. a. Priya was excited about her birthday, <u>therefore</u> she got up early.
   b. Kwame loves spicy food, <u>although</u> his sister Tiyana is not so keen.
   c. Latoya wanted to go because her friends were going, <u>although</u> she had a cold.
   d. <u>As a result of</u> her injured foot, Maya's coach made her rest, so her foot would heal.
2. Students' own sentences.
3. Students' own sentences using a different connective.
4. Students' own sentences adding more information before the connective.

Features of a playscript, page 9

Students' own playscript, including stage directions and character directions in the present tense.

Modal verbs of ability, obligation and advice, page 10

1.

Sentence	Advice	Obligation	Ability
My dad can juggle with six balls.			✓
We must buy the eggs for the recipe.		✓	
You ought to buy a gift for your sister.	✓		
You should brush your teeth before bed.	✓		
He could hold his breath for two minutes.			✓
I really have to leave for school.		✓	

2. a. The horse couldn't/could not jump over a tall fence.
   b. Shouldn't you/Should you not answer the door?
   c. Tell them they mustn't/ must not make lots of noise.
3. Students' own sentences.

Conditional sentences, page 11

1. a. second conditional
   b. second conditional
   c. third conditional
2. a. If I had more money, I would buy a boat.
   b. If she trained harder, she would win.
   c. If I spoke French, I would move to Paris.
   d. We would visit if we had more time.
3. a. If he had become a painter, he would have been famous.
   b. If she had stolen your pencil case, she would have admitted it by now.
   c. If you had been on time, we would've/would have seen the movie star.
   d. We would have been upset if he had left us out.
4. Students' own conditionals.

Unit 2 Sports

Live commentary, pages 14–15

1. None.
2. They lose possession of the ball.
3. The Reds
4. A moment of brilliance
5. The Blues
6. Students' own explanations.
7. skill
8. Students' own commentaries.

Emphasis and bias, pages 16–17

1. Students' own sentences.
2. Students' own sentences.

page 17

1.

	Biased	Unbiased
The Barracudas have lost three matches this season, but the Sharks haven't lost a single game.		✓
Our yummy new product, Choco Munchy, is the perfect start to your day.	✓	
Investing millions of dollars in the high-speed train line was a waste of money.	✓	
Researchers have found a connection between not sleeping enough and mood shifts.		✓

2. a. Students' own sentences.
   b. Students' own ideas.

A star athlete retires, page 18

1. The 37-year-old Jamaican sprinter Shelly-Ann Fraser-Pryce has announced that the Paris Games will be her fifth and final Olympics.
2. "My son needs me" "My husband and I have been together since before I won in 2008. He has sacrificed for me. We're a partnership, a team. And it's because of that support that I'm able to do the things that I have been doing for all these years. And I think I now owe it to them to do something else."
3. second place at Jamaica's Olympic trials in 2008; lead a Jamaican sweep in the 100 metres at the Beijing Games; first of her eight Olympic medals, four silvers and one bronze; ten gold medals at world championships, six individual championships – five in the 100 metres and one in the 200 metres; oldest woman to win the world title; won it again in 2022 at age 35.
4. Answers may vary but can include: will retire after Paris so she can spend more time with her family; We're a partnership, a team; she became the oldest woman to win the world title; she returned after the birth of her son

Questions about the text, page 19

1. Four
2. To spend more time with her family.
3. 2008
4. Total: 8
   Gold: 3
   Silver: 4
   Bronze: 1
5. At world championships.
6. (She was the oldest woman to) win the world title
7. They support each other.
8. Students' own ideas.

Quotations, page 20

1. a. She said, "I have enjoyed swimming since I was tiny."
   b. "The final match was the hardest. Things weren't going our way," he explained.
   c. "All good things come to an end," she remarked with a sigh. "Retiring isn't easy … but it feels right now."
2. a. The female cricketer said, "It was the greatest day of my career. I scored my first century."
   b. The male cyclist said, "I was unlucky. With two kilometres to go, the rear tyre blew."
   c. The female basketball player said, "I don't remember the final whistle. We were just all jumping and hugging. It was the best!"

Active and passive voices, page 21

1.

Sentence	Active	Passive
Aiden was given out by the umpire.		✓
Latoya ran the fastest time in the heats.	✓	
Kwame headed the ball back to the goalkeeper.	✓	
Maya has been selected to compete in the gymnastics championships.		✓

2. a. The umpire gave out Aiden.
   b. The fastest time in the heats was run (by Latoya).
3. Students' own ideas.
4. a. manager = subject; sell = action; player = object
   b. rugby = subject; is played = action; nations = object
   c. match = subject; was sent off = action; their captain = object
5. Students' own sentences.

Unit 3 Mother Nature

Personification, page 24

1. The aroma of the BBQ – crept up my nose.
   The palm trees – shook their heads in the wind.
   The ice-cream – called to me from the freezer.
   The paint brush – danced across the canvas.
   The traffic – crawled along the road.
   The gates – guarded the entrance to the house.
2. The aroma of the BBQ <u>crept up</u> my nose.
   The palm trees <u>shook</u> their heads in the wind.
   The ice-cream <u>called</u> to me from the freezer.
   The paint brush <u>danced</u> across the canvas.
   The traffic <u>crawled along</u> the road.
   The gates <u>guarded</u> the entrance to the house.
3. Students' own combinations.

Word choice and hyphens, page 25

1. Answers will vary.
2. a. My Spanish-speaking friend is a well-known singer.
   b. A robbery was foiled by a quick-witted passer-by.
   c. The long-eared alien returned to its time-travelling spaceship.
   d. His great-grandmother's favourite place was a hard-to-find café.
3. a. a small two-bedroom house
   b. a five-day journey
   c. a thirty-two-year-old woman
   d. a brown-eyed and long-haired dog

Improving writing through word choice, page 26

Students' own story openings.

The Monster in the Mountain, page 27

1. A volcano
2. Students' own explanations.
3. Lines will vary but may include: Her stony <u>face</u> has never betrayed; The stewing fury in her <u>belly</u>; That <u>veins</u> of fire throb and pulse and burrow; Under weather-beaten <u>skin</u>; snakes of lava slither from her cracked <u>skull</u>; When her spewing <u>jaws</u> have closed
4. Students' own explanations.
5. Students' own words.

Poetry review, page 28

1–6. Students' own answers and reviews.

Similes, page 29

1. The hail sounded <u>like a thousand little hammers</u> tapping on the roof. A flash light <u>as bright as the sun</u> illuminated everyone's faces for a split second. There was silence and darkness again until a few seconds later, thunder grumbled <u>like a monster's empty belly</u>. My sister, who was usually <u>as brave as a lion</u>, huddled next to Mum and hid her face from the storm. I was scared too. My mouth was <u>as dry as sand</u>. I went to sit next to my sister and held her hand.

2–3. Students' own ideas organised in paragraphs.

Metaphors, page 30

1. a. simile
   b. metaphor
   c. simile
   d. metaphor
2. a. The wind was an angry hissing snake.
   b. The melting snow was a tatty, dirty blanket.
   c. The midday sun was a golden coin.
   d. The long drought was a hand around the throat of the land.
3. Students' own metaphors.

Loanwords, page 31

1. Across: 2. phobia; 5. balcony; 7. tornado; 9. moped; 10. pearl
   Down: 1. robot; 3. banana; 4. lemon; 6. cookie; 8. noodle
2. Students' own sentences.

Unit 4 Suspense

Using senses for descriptive writing, page 34

1. Students' own ideas, using full sentences.

Adverbials, page 35

1. a. In the corner of the room, the grandfather clock was ticking.
   b. Tomorrow, Brianna was going to face a bigger challenge.
   c. Without making a sound, Anton approached the back door.
   d. Carefully, the agent cut the wires of the listening device.
2. Students' own sentences.
3. Students' own sentences.

Creating suspense using promise sentences, page 36

1. a. Kwame wished he hadn't overheard that secret that morning.
   c. If Latoya had answered the phone, then the trouble would never have started.
2. b. rang, would
   c. happened, wished
   d. have, foreseen
3. Students' own sentences.
4. Students' own sentences.

Building tension using questions, page 37

1. b. Was there a figure in the corner?
   c. Could we relax at last?
   d. Was she sensible to keep going?
2. a. Why
   b. How
   c. What/Who
3. a. isn't it
   b. will you
   c. wasn't she

4. a. Why aren't you answering me?
    b. There's something behind that door, isn't there?
    c. Do I want to go in that creepy, dark cellar?

Building tension and creating suspense, page 38

1. b, c, d, f, g, h
2. a. Creaking sound, right above our heads
    b. Silence, then, a muffled voice.
3. Students' own passages and stories.

Using ellipses and single dashes for suspense, page 39

1. Students' own dialogue lines.
2. a. The man began to say, "The problem is –"
    b. I tried to reply, "But none of this is my –"
3. a. It was just a bird calling in the forest – or was it?
    b. I can't play football after school – I have to help cook.
    c. She tried to phone her friend – she didn't answer.
4. Students' own sentences.

The Mirror Man, pages 40–41

1. Students tick all the features but ellipses, short sentences and sentence fragments.
2. Students' own choices and corresponding examples.
3. Students' own paragraphs.

Unit 5 Making a difference

Your ideas about the environment, page 44

1. Students' own ideas.
2. Students' own ideas.
3. Students' own ideas.

Making adjectives from nouns, page 45

1. musical, likely, legendary, selfish, ladylike
2. mountainous, famous, courageous, disastrous, photographic, artistic, energetic, climatic
3. a. useless
    b. painful
    c. comical
    d. noisy
4. a. universal
    b. plentiful
    c. historical
    d. ridiculous

Less common prefixes, page 46

1. a. against
    b. beyond
    c. large
2. a. postscript
    b. extraterrestrial
    c. monorail
3. a. The weather forecast was presented by a bilingual person.
    b. At midday today, the doctor gave the antidote to the poisoned players just before their semifinal.
4. Students' own sentences.

Persuasive writing, pages 47–48

Wording may vary:
1. Our beautiful beaches are a dangerous mess.
2. To use alternatives to plastic.
3. To introduce laws that force companies to significantly reduce their plastic usage and switch to eco-friendly materials
4. decompose
5. a. Sea turtles, fish and birds often mistake plastic for food./Plastic takes hundreds of years to decompose./There are many eco-friendly materials available today that can replace plastic in packaging and products.
    b. Answers will vary.
6. a. Answers will vary, for example: I am sure that you, like me, want to keep our beaches clean.
    b. Answers will vary, for example: It's persuasive because the writer is trying to make the reader feel they are both sensible people and therefore whatever the writer suggests will be what the reader wants to do too.

Features of a persuasive text, page 49

Students' own colour keys and examples.

Purpose, form, audience and tone, page 50

1. to persuade – make a reader agree with something
    to describe – share information about a topic with a reader
    to explain – tell a reader how something works
    to entertain – make a reader laugh
2. a. purpose: to inform/persuade/describe; audience: potential parents, students
    b. purpose: to entertain; audience: teenagers
3. a. a newspaper article   b. a letter
4. a. informal   b. formal   c. formal

Facts and opinions, page 51

1. a. opinion   b. fact
    c. opinion   d. fact
2. Facts: Yesterday, we visited the zoo. The zoo houses 150 species of animals from all around the world. The male weighs 2,300 kilograms. We saw a 5-metre-long Burmese python. There were parrots, toucans, peacocks and many other colourful birds. One of the zookeepers talked to us about the importance of conservation.

    Opinions: It was an incredible experience! One of the highlights was seeing the pair of rhinos. Watching these powerful creatures was truly mesmerising. The zoo also has a state-of-the-art reptile house. Even though it was behind glass, it was still frightening. One of the parts I didn't like so much was the bird house. I felt a bit sad for them because I thought there wasn't enough space to fly around properly. All those birds should be free in the wild.
3. Answers will vary.

Unit 6 Creating characters

Participle adjectives, page 54

1. a. boring
   b. exhausting
   c. uplifted
   d. terrified

2.

Verb	Present participle	Past participle
wear	wearing	worn
lose	losing	lost
freeze	freezing	frozen
break	breaking	broken
tire	tiring	tired
excite	exciting	excited
hide	hiding	hidden
forget	forgetting	forgot
irritate	irritating	irritated
embarrass	embarrassing	embarrassed
satisfy	satisfying	satisfied

3. Students' own sentences

Describing appearance and personality, page 55

1. a. magnetic – entrancing
   b. morose – gloomy
   c. hoarse – husky
   d. messy – wild

2. a. compassionate – understanding
      stubborn – obstinate
      considerate – thoughtful
      foolish – witless
   b. bold – timid
      placid – agitated
      generous – miserly
      humble – arrogant

3. Answers will vary.

4. Students' own descriptions.

Character descriptions, page 56

Students' own descriptions.

Writing a backstory, page 57

Students' own backstories.

Reading for explicit and implicit information, pages 58–59

1. a. He stuck out a hand to catch it, but in doing so, he elbowed a diner in the back of the head.
   b. a teaspoon
   c. grilled snapper
   d. (Dijon) mustard

2. a. Oliver: server; Celeste: cook/chef
   b–e. Students' own answers, with reasons.

Direct speech, page 60

1. a. Spoken words: "Do you know the way to the harbour?" Reporting clause: the old man asked.
   b. Reporting clause: I replied. Spoken words: "It's just down the hill and to the left. I can show you the way."
   c. Spoken words: "Thank you," and "that would be very helpful." Reporting clause: he said with a smile.

2. a. "That was one of the best meals I've ever had," Mum announced.
   b. Dad nodded and remarked, "Yes, it was fantastic, wasn't it?"
   c. "Would you like to see the dessert menu?" asked the server.
   d. "I'm so full I shouldn't," replied Dad, "but yes, please!"

3. a. Maya said, "You forgot to tell me about the test!"
   b. "Why is it my job to remind you?" asked Nancy.
   c. "I'm going to fail," groaned Maya, "and it's all your fault!"

4. Students' own dialogues.

What other characters think, page 61

2. a. What Larry's friends most likely think of him: brilliant, worthy
   b. What his opponents most likely think of him: disloyal, misguided, arrogant, greedy, boastful, ungrateful
   c. What his friends and opponents might both think: determined, talented

3. a.–c. Students' own explanations.

Unit 7 Exploring food

Food experiences, page 64

1. Students' own descriptions.
2. Students' own experiences.

Phrasal verbs, page 65

1. a. get up
   b. get off
   c. get out of
   d. get along with

2. a. clean up
   b. fill, up
   c. shown up, give up
   d. called, up; hung up

3. hold off – delay
   let down – disappoint
   give away – donate
   use up – exhaust
   leave out – omit

4. Students' own sentences.

Silent letters and unstressed vowels, page 66

1. a. difference
   b. poisonous
   c. desperate
   d. general
   e. vegetable
   f. dictionary
   g. cemetery
   h. separate
2. a. Students underline the letter 'a' in '–ally'.
   b. Wording may vary: The letter a is silent at the '–ally' ending of a word.
   c. Students underline the letter 'h' in each word.
   d. Wording may vary: The letter 'h' is silent after the 'c' in each word.
3. The knight climbed up to the castle on the island. He was in disguise and the hour was late, so he doubted he would be stopped. He drew his sword and entered the building. From the library, he descended into the frightening tomb. A solemn hymn was echoing. No one seemed interested in him. It was a miserable scene.

Should fast food have an age restriction? Questions about the text, pages 67–68

1. requirement
2. fat, sugar and salt
3. first paragraph – opening statement
   second paragraph – arguments against
   third paragraph – arguments for
   fourth paragraph – conclusion
4. Students' own explanations.
5. It would not be fair for some people.
   People should make their own choices.
   Banning fast food could make it more desirable.
6. Students' own words but they should focus on education, as nutrition programmes in schools can help children learn about how to eat healthily and have balanced diets.
7. Students' own answers.

Impersonal voice and quantifiers, page 69

1. a. Many people claim that sugar is bad for your teeth.
   b. It is known by dentists that bacteria feed on the sugar and create acids.
2. a. few
   b. every
   c. every
   d. few
3. a. much
   b. many
   c. much
   d. many
4. Students' own sentences.
5. Students' own impersonal voice sentences.

Connectives in balanced arguments, page 70

1. Students' own colours for reinforcing connectives: Firstly, Secondly, In addition, Lastly, Furthermore, Finally,
   contrasting connectives: despite, By contrast, However, so,
   cause and effect connectives: because, For this reason, since, Hence
2. a. As a result/Consequently/Therefore
   b. now that/since
   c. as/since
   d. even though
   e. as/since
   f. As a result/Consequently/Therefore

Colons and semi-colons, page 71

1. Students tick: We have plenty to make a fruit salad: bananas, mango, pineapple and papaya.
   I had to leave school early: I was feeling unwell after eating lunch.
   He gave us some good advice: "The grilled snapper is the best on the island."
2. a. These are my favourite things: ginger biscuits, key lime pie and coleslaw.
   b. She said the following: "Cheese is wonderful."
   c. My food is burned: I forgot to take it out of the oven.
3. Students underline the clause before the semi-colon in one colour, and the clause after it, in another colour:
   a. Aiden likes fast food; Priya prefers traditional food.
   b. Kwame went to the dentist; meanwhile, Tiyana went shopping.
   c. Omar's sister is called Amina; Femi is Aiden's sister.

Unit 8 Moving on

A sensory memory, page 74

Students' own descriptions.

Oxymorons, page 75

1. a. same difference
   b. small crowd
   c. pretty ugly
2. random order
   minor crisis
   deafening silence
   only choice
   least favourite
   working holiday
   crash landing
   seriously funny
   old news
   unbiased opinion
3. Students' own paragraphs.

A review of literary devices, pages 76–77

Literary device name	Definition	Example
simile	a comparison using *like* or *as*	Her eyes were dark as coals.
oxymoron	when two words are put together that have opposing or contradictory meanings	This burger is disgustingly delicious!
hyperbole	an exaggeration for emphasis or humour	I've told you that a million times.
metaphor	a direct comparison of two things without using *like* or *as*	His face is a book.
onomatopoeia	words that match the sound they describe	Buzz, whizz, bang, crash!
idiom	a well-known phrase that has a non-literal meaning	She let the cat out of the bag.
assonance	the repetition of vowel sounds in nearby words	I might try to fly my kite.
symbolism	an object, action or name that represents something more than its literal meaning	a dove (peace), a phoenix (rebirth), a photograph (a memory)
personification	giving human characteristics to non-human things	The trees danced in the wind.
alliteration	the repetition of consonant sounds at the beginning of nearby words	The racing runner returned rapidly.

Memories from school, page 78

Students' own memories and pictures.

School memories poem planner, page 79

Students' own memories.

Aspiration balloon, page 80

Students' own aspirations.

Punctuating a letter, page 81

321 Bay Lane
Sunny Beach
19 October, 2025

Dear Grandma,

I hope you are well. I have some exciting news to share with you. Yesterday, I competed in my first ever karate competition and guess what, I won.

The competition was at the brand-new dojo in Sunny Bay. I was so nervous at first because all the other kids were older and more experienced than me. However, I remembered how you always tell me to believe in myself.

Somehow, I reached the final. I was worried that my opponent's footwork and speed were better than mine. Although he hit me a few times, I kept my self-control. I managed to score the final point and I'd beaten a twelve-year-old boy. I was so proud. I wish you could've been there to see it but I know you were cheering for me from home.

Mum and Dad took lots of pictures. I'll send some to you soon. I can't wait to visit you and show you my medal. I miss you so much.

Lots of love,

Melissa

Types of compound nouns, page 82

1.

C1 + A5	weekend	C5 + A1	without
B5 + E4	time capsule	B3 + D4	high school
C4 + E2	bedroom	D1 + A3	downstairs
A2 + D3	salad dressing	C3 + A4	no one
B4 + E3	somebody	E1 + C2	videogame
E5 + B1	washing machine	B2 + D2 + D5	nevertheless

2. a. cell phones
   b. commanders-in-chief
   c. report cards
   d. take-offs
   e. daughters-in-law
3. Students' own sentences.

Unit 9 Preparing for tests

How to help your child prepare for a test, pages 84–85

1. The text is about preparing your child for a test.
2. To inform parents/carers how they can help children before and during tests.
3. It is aimed at parents/carers of children taking tests. It directly addresses this audience by asking the question 'How can we, as parents and carers, make …' including them by using 'we', and goes on to use the address 'you'/'your' throughout.
4. guide/work through
5. Because tests can be stressful and children and their families may feel under pressure.
6. Answers will vary but may include: create, stay, communicate, talk, and so on.
7. Imperative verbs are direct and to the point – the writer uses them as they are giving a list of instructions.
8. 1. They should eat lots of protein and healthy fats.
   2. Drink lots of water.
9. It is essential for wellbeing as physical activity helps children relax and switch off (especially if they can be outside).
10. Answers will vary depending on how useful students find the text. Accept answers where opinion is backed up by two reasons from the text.

Letter writing, page 86

Students' own letters.

Test-style practice questions, page 87

Spelling, page 87

1. c. really
2. a. irreplaceable
3. b. happened
4. c. potatoes
5. a. impossible
6. b. untied

Grammar, page 88

1. a. would
2. c. can
3. b. me
4. c. hopes
5. a. who
6. b. because
7. a. themselves

Grammar, page 89

1. b. had known
2. c. was wrapping
3. a. don't

1. Nouns: hospital, arm; Verbs: needed, go, had broken
2. Nouns: teacher, sports, trainers; Verbs: asked, could, be excused, had forgotten
1. Maya told her aunt that she would try to come over after school to help her clean the church.
2. The teacher warned the children that if they didn't hurry up, they would miss the bus.
3. Omar said that he had already finished the maths questions Mrs Hosein had given them.

Reading, page 90

1. A party for Grade 6 leavers
2. At Eden Park
3. All St Joseph's leavers in Grade 6 and their friends and family (up to 4 people).
4. Because it is a party to say goodbye to the Grade 6 leavers and represents the end of something.
5. Students' own answers. Answers may include:
   1. Use of exclamation marks to make it sound fun (e.g. Party in the park!). 2. Use of rhetorical-type questions to make leavers feel included (e.g. Do you like games? Music?... Thought so!). 3. Attractive design of invite which makes it seem like an event not to be missed.
6. Answers will vary depending on what students think the event will be like. Accept answers where opinion is backed up by a reason from the text.

Sweet and Low, page 91

1. b. the wind
2. a. alliteration
3. b. the father
4. c. boat
5. a. calm and hopeful

Writing a short story, page 92

Students' own stories. For guidance on marking test-type writing tasks please see page 42 of this Teacher's Guide.

Listening activity transcripts

Unit 2 page 21

Live commentary, Part 1: A sprint race

Commentator: And they're off! The athletes are out of the blocks cleanly. No false start the second time. The current champion, Clarke, in Lane 5, makes a lightning start. He's up slightly on his opponents. The crowd is roaring their favourite on. The runners, they're coming round the bend. It's tight. Just over halfway now. And here he goes! Clarke pulls ahead. He's digging deep, long strides, arms pumping. Fifty to go. Here comes Brown, the former record holder, on the outside! Brown is closing! Clarke's tensing up! It's anyone's race! Across the line. It's Clarke, or is it? It's Clarke, I think. By a hair. No, we will have to wait and see. It's a photo finish. What a race! Brown was trailing halfway down the straight. Rarely have I seen the champion chased down like that. Clarke is crouched over, sucking in air, staring up at the stadium screen. He wants to know – ten thousand people want to know – has he won for a third time? The wait must be agonising. And there it is! The results are in … and we have a new champion!

Unit 2 page 22

Live commentary, Part 2: A cricket match

Commentator 1: That is an incredible shot! She's completely taken charge out there, hasn't she?

Commentator 2: Absolutely, she's showing real class and composure at the crease. And this could be her moment. She's on 96. In comes the bowler, who overpitches, and she drives majestically through the covers for four. There it is! A century off 50 deliveries exactly. What a phenomenal achievement!

Commentator 1: Incredible! She's been in destructive form from the very first ball of this innings. Shot selection, placement, power, everything – effortless.

Commentator 3: For those of you who love your stats as much as we do, that's the fifth fastest century of all time. A truly remarkable performance from the veteran.

Commentator 2: How about how she's timed the ball?

Commentator 3: Impeccable.

Commentator 2: The ball has been flying off her bat like a rocket. It's times like this when you feel sorry for the bowlers. They just can't seem to find a way to slow the flood of runs.

Commentator 1: Indeed, we are witnessing batting at its finest. There were some doubts about her after such a long injury layoff, but she's proving why she's still one of the best batters in the world. It's moments like these that remind us why we love this game. What a privilege it is to watch such talent.

Commentator 3: Just a reminder that the game remains in the balance here. What's important is the win. It would be quite something if she could bat through and lead her team to victory, wouldn't it?

Commentator 2: Well, she's so full of confidence right now, I think she might clinch it for them. The bowling team simply must take some wickets, but their heads are down.

Commentator 1: Oh, and this might be their chance! She's clubbed that straight up in the air … and the ball's gone right down the fielder's throat at mid-wicket. Look at the relief on the fielders' faces.

Commentator 3: Yes, they're ecstatic. They'll be keen to put pressure on the new batter, who will no doubt be nervous. Game on again! It's all to play for now.

Unit 4 page 55

A night in the jungle, Part 1

It is the holidays, and Omar and his brother Ahmed are staying with their grandparents, who run an ecolodge in the rainforest for tourists. Omar has not been to the lodge before. He and his brother are sharing a room. After a long journey and first day, Omar is ready for bed.

Omar closed his eyes. It had been such an amazing first day. Images from the day played across the insides of his eyelids like a film: the needle-like spikes on a thick vine; a toucan high in the canopy with a neon-yellow bill; crystal-clear water cascading between smooth stones. Omar sighed.

"What's up?" said Ahmed, who was sitting up in his own bed reading.

"I'm so tired," replied Omar, "but I can't get to sleep."

"Uh-huh," muttered Ahmed. "Try closing your eyes."

"Wow, thanks for the advice," said Omar. He turned over in bed and tried to get comfortable. He shut his eyes again and gradually the wonderful but distracting memories from the day began to fragment and fade until there was just darkness.

Sometime later, Omar's eyes flickered open. The room was dark, except for a strip of orange light seeping under the bottom of the door from the lamp on the porch. For a terrifying few moments, Omar had no idea where he was. The feeling wrenched him out of sleep completely. He sat up with a start. In the gloom, he could just make out the bed next to him. The sheet was thrown aside. The bed was empty.

"Ahmed?" he said. His voice was croaky with sleep. No reply. At that moment, listening for signs of his brother, Omar became aware that the night was full of strange noises: bursts of buzzing and eerie whines like half-broken machines; sudden squawks and low, mournful howls. Perhaps it was all the nocturnal noise that had woken him. He began to imagine the kind of creatures that were filling the dark jungle air with their calls and warnings and threats. What was that rasping, clicking sound? Was it some giant beetle the size of a plate gnashing its fangs together? Where was the sound coming from? Was it outside? Had Ahmed gone out and the beetle got in? Was it under the bed, orange light dancing off its huge, shiny, staring, beady eyes?

"Ahmed!" Omar called out.

No reply.

Unit 7 page 116

New food: Aiden, Kwame, Maya and Priya talk about food

Hi, I'm Aiden. Fast food is the best! I would have a burger, onion rings, mac pie and a shake every day if I was allowed. I love how it all tastes so salty and sweet, and the smell just makes my mouth water. I don't like salad. Cucumbers taste bitter and tomatoes are full of watery juice. Lettuce is floppy and tasteless. I like nature and the countryside, but it doesn't taste good! My parents say I'm a fussy eater because I don't like trying new things, especially traditional foods like cou-cou and ackee. But now I've started eating tuna and eggs because they're good for your muscles and bones, and I want to be fit. I don't like spicy food, so I've never tried curry chicken.

Hi, I'm Kwame. I think I'm happy to eat most things. There are some traditional foods that we have at home that I've never liked. We used to have callaloo for breakfast every day, but my grandma always stewed it so long it went mushy. I love other traditional foods though like jerk chicken and pepperpot. I like fast food too, even though my Granny Grace doesn't approve. My favourites are chicken quesadillas and a fruit split ice-cream. I will never eat guacamole again. No! It was green and lumpy and reminded me of my grandma's callaloo!

Hello, I'm Maya. I'm always hungry because I do so much exercise, so I will try anything. I don't mind if it's traditional or new: green bananas, garlic bread, fungee, conch fritters, burrito bowls, all of it. I've tried iguana stew and pigtail soup. And I love spicy peppers like scotch bonnets. I think they have a tangy, fruity flavour. Tamarind balls are the best. I always have some after gym practice. I love the sticky, savoury tamarind with the sweet brown sugar.

Hi, I'm Priya. My diet is mostly vegetarian, and I prefer traditional food. I think it is because I spend so much time cooking with my mum. My grandma taught me how to make rotis when I was little. I'm not keen on takeaway food. It always looks nicer in the adverts than it is. Some people love fried chicken, but it's too fatty. It even smells greasy to me!

Glossary

A

addictive makes you want more
antagonist the main opponent in a story
awareness knowledge that something exists

B

bioluminescent light made by a living creature
burdening something that causes difficulty, worry or hard work

C

campus the buildings and lands of a university
cascade to pour rapidly
confront to challenge someone face to face
convenient easy and useful

D

degree a qualification from university
distract to interrupt someone's attention

E

eerie strange and frightening

F

falter to lose strength
fiddle a violin
finance the way people use money

G

gabble to talk rapidly and unclearly
guttural a sound produced at the back of the throat

H

hind back
hulking heavily built

J

journal a publication about a particular subject
justice to treat somebody or something fairly

L

luxurious expensive and comfortable

M

motivate to be the reason for doing something
musty smelling old and wet

N

nutrients substances from food that help you live and grow

P

parched dried out
plumage covering of feathers
processed treated or prepared
profile someone's face from the side
protagonist the main character in a story
pursue to chase

R

ravine a narrow valley with steep sides
relatable someone you can understand or feel sympathy for
resonate to fill with sound through vibrations
retain to keep or continue to have something

S

saunter to walk in a slow, relaxed manner
serpentine the curving shape of a snake
sluggish moving more slowly than usual
spontaneously naturally, without planning
stalactite a column of rock hanging from a cave roof
sustainable something that does little damage and can keep going

T

tail to follow someone secretly
threshold entrance
trespassing entering without permission

Playscript planner

Use this grid to note down and organise your ideas.

Main characters (no more than three)	
Additional characters (maximum two, roles and personalities)	
Plot (upcoming events or remainder of the story)	
Scene notes (characters, setting, stage directions)	
Scene notes (characters, setting, stage directions)	
Scene notes (characters, setting, stage directions)	

© Oxford University Press 2025. No sharing, copying or adaptation of materials permitted except by purchasing schools.

Newspaper write-up report planner

Use this grid to plan your write-up of your newspaper report.

Name of person the report is about:
What are some basic facts about this person?
How will you introduce this person?
What are the main achievements of this person?
What do you want to convey (let people know) about their personality?
Which quotations help tell your interviewee's story most strongly?
How will you end your write-up? (quotation/summary)

© Oxford University Press 2025. No sharing, copying or adaptation of materials permitted except by purchasing schools.

Mother Nature poem planner

Use this grid to note down and organise your ideas.

What aspect of Mother Nature is your poem about?	
What are you trying to express about it?	
Personification ideas	
Simile and metaphor ideas	
Other figurative language (for example, onomatopoeia, alliteration)	
Synonyms and antonyms (for contrast)	
Rhyming words if required	
Powerful and interesting words (for example, hyphenated words, loanwords)	

© Oxford University Press 2025. No sharing, copying or adaptation of materials permitted except by purchasing schools.

Suspense story planner

Use this planning grid to come up with and organise your suspense story.

Who are your four characters?
What is the setting? (location, materials, weather, etc.)
Why do your characters go there?
What challenge do they face? (problem, danger, obstacle, enemy, etc.)
How do your characters react to the challenge?
What is the most tense moment?
What are the consequences for your characters at the end?

© Oxford University Press 2025. No sharing, copying or adaptation of materials permitted except by purchasing schools.

Persuasive letter planner

Use this grid to plan your letter.

Who are you writing to?		
Introduction: Purpose? Why are you writing to them? What will you tell them about?		
Problem: What problem needs solving?	Opinions:	Facts and evidence:
Solution: What solution is there? How can they and others help?	Opinions:	Facts and evidence:
Closing: Thank them and restate your overall opinion and call to action.		

© Oxford University Press 2025. No sharing, copying or adaptation of materials permitted except by purchasing schools.

Character story planner

Use this grid to gather and organise ideas for your character in your story. In the scenes, you should introduce and challenge your character.

How will you introduce your character? (who, what, where, when, why)
How will you challenge your character?
How will they react? (in keeping with your full description)
What happens in the first scene?
What happens next?
What happens after that?
Key things to show about your character's appearance
Key things to show about your character's backstory, personality and motivations

© Oxford University Press 2025. No sharing, copying or adaptation of materials permitted except by purchasing schools.

Balanced argument planner

Use this grid to plan your balanced argument.

Title (write a question):
Opening statement (introduce the subject):

Arguments with evidence, examples and facts	
For	Against
For	Against
For	Against

Conclusion (summarise the arguments):

Language features (tick the ones you will try to use):

impersonal voice phrases	☐	a range of quantifiers	☐
a range of connectives	☐	colons and semi-colons	☐

© Oxford University Press 2025. No sharing, copying or adaptation of materials permitted except by purchasing schools.

Use this grid to note down and organise your ideas.

What memories are you including?	
'Seeing' ideas	
'Hearing' ideas	
'Smelling' ideas	
'Tasting' ideas	
'Feeling' ideas	
Poetic devices and synonym ideas	

© Oxford University Press 2025. No sharing, copying or adaptation of materials permitted except by purchasing schools.